# SURRENDERED SEXUALITY

# SURRENDERED SEXUALITY

How Knowing Jesus Changes . . . Everything

Dr. Juli Slattery

MOODY PUBLISHERS
CHICAGO

Some of the content in chapter 3 has been paraphrased from the author's *God, Sex, and Your Marriage* (Moody, 2022). A few statements have been adapted from the author's writing for FocusontheFamily.org and Boundless.org.



All emphasis in Scripture has been added.

Names and details of some stories have been changed to protect the privacy of individuals. Some accounts are compilations.

Edited by Pamela Joy Pugh
Interior design: Puckett Smartt
Cover design: Brittany Schrock
Cover image: Cover gradient color copyright © 2024 by Jordan Steranka, courtesy of Unsplash.
Author photo: The Cannons Photography

ISBN: 978-0-8024-3517-0

Originally delivered by fleets of horse-drawn wagons, the affordable paperbacks from D. L. Moody's publishing house resourced the church and served everyday people. Now, after more than 125 years of publishing and ministry, Moody Publishers' mission remains the same—even if our delivery systems have changed a bit. For more information on other books (and resources) created from a biblical perspective, go to www.moodypublishers.com or write to:

Moody Publishers
820 N. LaSalle Boulevard
Chicago, IL 60610

1 3 5 7 9 10 8 6 4 2

*Printed in the United States of America*

This book is dedicated to the women and men
who helped me write it. Over decades of ministry,
I've been taught by dear ones who have wrestled with God
and asked every question this book represents.
You have shown me through your lives
how to relentlessly pursue a Jesus who
truly does change everything.

# CONTENTS

# Let's Get Started

Hi friend!

Thank you for picking up this book. Before you dive in, I'd like to share a few things with you.

First, I wrote this book with Christians in mind. By "Christians," I am referring to people who have chosen to give their lives to God by believing and trusting in Jesus Christ to save them from their sin. A Christian is called by Jesus to live a different kind of life—to give their lives to know Jesus and bring glory to God.

If you have not given your life to God, *Surrendered Sexuality* may not make sense to you and may even be offensive. I understand that. I also acknowledge that Christians don't always live as we should. Your deepest pain and disappointment might have come from someone who is a Christian. That's why I wrote this book: to guide and challenge my brothers and sisters to surrender to the work of Jesus in their lives related to sexual issues, including how we treat people.

Second, this book is imperfect. When I revisit it ten years from now, chances are I'll find some things I'd like to express differently. My heart behind this book is for us to pursue Jesus together, as I am on my own journey of surrender with the Lord. If you take steps toward a deeper relationship with Jesus as you read these words, then I praise God.

Finally, surrender is a lifelong journey in which we each need encouragement from other Christians. I have included application exercises and passages to study at the end of each chapter that can help you process what you've read and apply it to your own relationship with the Lord. I strongly encourage you to go through *Surrendered* with a friend or a small group. As I wrote the book, several pilot groups went through the content together. What transpired in their discussions and sharing was powerful and helpful. We need one another for encouragement, perspective, and comfort.

One more thing—some people have asked me what I mean by "sexuality." Typically, we think of sexuality as the same thing as sex. Sexuality is the aspect of our humanity that causes us to desire intimate connections with others. It means far more than the act of sex. This includes our gender, physiological bodies, and psychological experiences. So as we look at surrendering our sexuality, we will be addressing much more than sexual behavior.

I have no idea what you might be bringing into this conversation of sexuality and Jesus. Whatever burdens, questions, and wounds come with you, I pray that the Lord, by His Spirit, will meet you in your seeking.

CHAPTER 1

# What Is Surrendered Sexuality?

Sex is never just about sex. It certainly wasn't for Shelly.

Her childhood began in an idyllic small town with a stable and loving family, but when she was seven, everything began to unravel as Shelly's dad was injured and unable to work. He started drinking, which led to an affair. When Shelly was eight, her older brother began molesting her; at age ten, her oldest sister ran away. Desperately wanting to hold her family together, Shelly hid the secret of what her brother had been doing to her.

Shelly was invited to a Vacation Bible School and was comforted to hear of Jesus' love for her. Then she attended Sunday school for a few short weeks where she learned about sin and realized that what her brother was doing to her was wrong. Though she was only ten, she wanted to please God, and Shelly courageously told her brother he could no longer do to her what he was doing. The abuse stopped.

The seed that God planted that summer never grew beyond an initial decision to trust God. Over the years, Shelly began to view Jesus as a faraway God looking down on her with disgust and disappointment for her sexual brokenness.

Shelly married when she was nineteen. Three years into marriage she was unfaithful for the first of many times. This was a behavior she found herself unable to break free of, though she had a loving husband and two children. But finally at thirty-seven, she felt trapped in sin and overwhelming shame. Believing there was no way out, Shelly determined to take her life.

People like my friend Shelly are the reason I write, speak, and podcast about sexuality.

✦ ✦ ✦

I wonder how you are feeling as you begin reading. Maybe your experience of God and sexuality is a confusing and emotionally charged journey. Maybe you know that God created sexuality and that it's supposed to be a good thing, but your experience of this "good gift," like Shelly's, has been one of pain, shame, and questions.

When you look around, it can seem as if everyone else has their lives together. Could anyone else be suffering or enslaved as you are? Where are the spaces to talk about your erotic dreams, your same-sex desire, your sexless marriage, or your porn addiction? Who is safe enough to hold your questions, your anger, and your trauma?

As Christians, we need to understand that sexuality is not primarily a *cultural* problem. It is a very personal spiritual terrain that plays out against the backdrop of culture.

This book is about your real questions and challenges in the arena of sexuality. We are going to get personal as we examine sensitive and painful subjects like sexual desire, loneliness, pornography, betrayal, lust, and brokenness. So let me share a little about why I care so much about this topic.

## A BIT OF BACKGROUND

My parents became committed followers of Jesus Christ when I was a baby. When God met them, they were in the middle of their own life and marriage crisis and Jesus changed everything. My earliest memories are of Bible studies in our home, and of going to church twice on Sundays and once on Wednesdays. I have had my own relationship with Jesus since I was a small child. I even attended Christian schools all the way through earning my master's degree. As an adult, I became a clinical psychologist with an emphasis on marriage and women's issues.

Even with all that spiritual heritage, biblical and psychological training, my education did not prepare me for most of what I will share with you throughout these pages. The extent of my understanding of Christian sexuality was this: God created sex for marriage and to make babies. Don't mess it up by having sex outside of marriage, dressing immodestly, or watching R-rated movies. When Mike and I got married, I had little to no preparation and nowhere to turn when we ran into problems in our sex life. I felt even less equipped to deal with the challenges of biblical sexuality in ministry, not to mention navigating these conversations as a mother of three sons.

***Sexuality is never a neutral issue in our relationship with God.***

While I don't know what you are personally walking through, I do know what it is like to love God and study the Bible, but still to feel like none of that practically helps you in one of the most painful, vulnerable, and confusing areas of your life.

In 2012, God dramatically called me into this ministry of biblical sexuality. To be transparent, I had no idea what I was saying yes to. I have learned more than I have taught and have been deeply impacted by the pain and wrestling sexuality represents for many of my brothers and sisters in Christ.

I am more committed and passionate than ever about the work God has called me to do, and here's why: Sexuality is never a neutral issue in our relationship with God. Our questions, our trauma, our longings, and our disappointment will either eventually draw us away from God or draw us to Him.

## THE STRUGGLES ARE REAL

I want to introduce you to just a few of the people I've come to know over the last decade, all who have a relationship with God through Jesus Christ and each one in a crisis of faith around sexuality.

---

Devon is a pastor who loves Jesus. He is also a man who has battled pornography and sexual addiction since he was a young teenager. Devon's wife, Amy, was devastated to discover her husband's porn use. Amy had her own battle with a low sex drive and painful intercourse. For a few years, the couple stopped having sex altogether. Their church congregation had no idea of the pain and shame they carried around this aspect of their relationship. While Devon knew he needed to include sexual topics in his preaching rotation, he couldn't bring himself to do so because of his own private struggles and shame.

---

When Noah hit puberty, he heard his friends talking about the pretty girls and joked about who they wanted to have sex with. Noah couldn't identify. He could never tell his buddies that his attraction was not to girls, but to other guys. He was a Christian, and in church homosexuality was only discussed as a horrible sin, so he concluded that he must be a terrible mistake. Noah has been honest with a few friends about his same-sex desires, but struggles to accept that he will live a life of loneliness without marriage and children.

---

---

Chantelle and Rich both grew up in the evangelical church and gave their lives to Jesus as teenagers. High school sweethearts, they married young and couldn't wait to enjoy sex. But as they began their marriage, memories of past sexual trauma and exploitation haunted Chantelle. She endured years of flashbacks, disordered eating, and sexual confusion. Through counseling, Chantelle began to work through her trauma, yet she still had no desire for sex. Rich, a godly man, feels like he's been cheated out of a sex life. He struggles between trying to love his wife and anger that his own desires have been so neglected.

---

Angie was raised in a Christian home and attended a conservative Christian college. Every talk she's ever heard about Christian sexuality has pointed to marriage. Angie desperately wants to be loved and to have a God-honoring way to channel her sexual desire. Yet she is twenty-nine and still single. She's angry at God for not meeting her needs for love and sex.

---

As you read these stories, you may find glimpses of yourself. Without question, you've seen the description of someone you deeply care about. Even if you are not in the middle of a crisis around sexuality, you probably have questions, confusion, and areas of doubt.

I could tell you many more stories about young adults convinced they were born in the wrong bodies, parents heartbroken by a child's sexual choices, and sexual assault victims wading through decades of despair and brokenness.

I care about your sexuality because I care about your relationship with God, and I have learned that they will always be linked. Our sexual wounds, questions, and longings tap into our wrestling with God. Is He good? Is He trustworthy? Does He see me? To ignore your sexual wounds, step over your sexual pain, or dismiss your sexual questions will eventually tear away at your love and commitment to the Lord Jesus Christ. I really don't want that to happen!

## WHAT DOES IT MEAN TO BE A CHRISTIAN?

You might think of a Christian as someone who prays, attends church, and lives by a certain moral code. That's not the right definition. The word *Christian* literally means "little anointed ones" or "little Christs." Being a Christian is not joining a religion or a people group that obeys a list of rules. To be a Christian means that you have exchanged your life for the life of Jesus Christ. Jesus doesn't just want converts, but disciples (see Matt. 28:19–20). Christianity is not just "asking Jesus into your heart," but the wholehearted pursuit of what it means to follow God with every aspect of your life.

One day, Jesus was asked, "What is the greatest commandment?" He responded with the commandment that every Israelite would have recited in morning prayer: "Love the Lord your God with all your heart and with all your soul and with all your mind." Then Jesus added another commandment, "Love your neighbor as yourself."

Do you notice that there is nothing specifically about your sexuality included in these commandments? Nothing about avoiding porn, being straight, or saving sex for marriage? What Jesus said next tells us why: "All the Law and the Prophets hang on these two commandments" (Matt. 22:36–40).

In other words, God calls you not simply to obey Him, but to give yourself—all your heart, soul, and mind—over to Him. The word *all* means *all*. If you have accepted Jesus Christ as your Savior, that means He is worthy of being your Lord. Your life no longer belongs to you as it once did. The only rational response to Jesus' sacrifice is for your whole life to come under His love, His authority, and His power.

Most of us would readily admit that even though we know our lives belong to Jesus, we don't fully live that way. While the blood of Jesus forgives all of our sins, the Christian journey involves a progressive process of giving Him all of our life. Even if you've trusted in Christ for your salvation, there are likely portions of your life that you're just not quite sure what to do with. And so we can end up feeling like we compartmentalize the parts of us that are more difficult to bring to Jesus.

In my own personal and ministry experience, I have learned that sexuality is very often one of these "compartments":

> We have nagging questions about sex the Bible doesn't seem to satisfactorily answer.
> We have sin struggles that won't go away.
> We have shame and wounds that still haunt us.

Living a compartmentalized Christian life may seem like it's working for a season, but it goes completely against what it means to love, obey, and trust God as our Savior and Lord. Between you and God there may be a great big invisible wall that just might have something to do with sex. A wall like:

> How could a good God tell people they can't marry the person they love?
> I just can't understand why God allowed me to be sexually abused.
> Doesn't God know how lonely I am? Why doesn't He bring me a soulmate?
> If God is anything like the people who say they represent Him, I can't trust Him.
> I feel like I have to choose between God and loving my transgender child.
> I feel so much shame for what I've done (and continue to struggle with). I don't think God could ever fully accept me as I am.
> Why would God want me to stay in a marriage that feels unfulfilling?

What have you done with that wall? Maybe you've tried not to think about it. Or perhaps you've tried to break through it by working really hard at living by God's standards. You may have even had some success in all that trying.

But here's the truth. God doesn't want your relationship with Him to be centered on working really hard to please Him.

The call to follow Jesus is a call of surrender.

## WHAT DOES IT MEAN TO SURRENDER?

*Webster* defines surrender this way: "To give oneself up into the power of another."[1]

Surrender is not a very popular concept in our day. To most of us, surrendering suggests the picture of giving up or losing. People surrender when they have exhausted every other option and resign themselves to something they never wanted to do in the first place.

Maybe this is what you are thinking as you consider surrendering your sexuality to the Lord. The Bible puts surrender in an entirely different light. A Christian doesn't surrender because he or she has no better options, but rather because only by surrendering can we find our true meaning and purpose in life.

God requires our surrender not because of what He wants to take from us, but what He so desires to give. Picture your life as if it were a container. Your life only has so much space. Any ounce that is given to water, for example, cannot be filled with oil. One displaces the other. In the same way, our lives can only be filled with the presence and the power of God to the extent that we surrender what we currently live for.

***The bottom line is this: We will never surrender to a God we can't trust.***

Surrender is when we no longer strive to be in control, asking for God's help to do what *we* think is best. Instead, we turn our lives over to Him. This is what tears down that wall between you and God. When we surrender our sexuality, the wounds, the questions, and the longings become the place where we invite God into the deepest, most intimate parts of who we are, and we discover Him.

One of the most well-known passages of surrender is found in Paul's letter to the Romans.

> Therefore, I urge you, brothers and sisters, in view of God's mercy, to offer your bodies as a living sacrifice, holy and pleasing to God—this is your true and proper worship. (Rom. 12:1)

The first word in this verse is "therefore." Whenever we see that word, we need to ask, "What is the 'therefore' *there for*?" It's referring to something the author has previously written. Backing up a few verses to Romans 11:33–36, we find Paul praising God for His plans, His power, and His wisdom that are so far beyond our understanding:

> Oh, the depth of the riches of the wisdom and knowledge of God!
>     How unsearchable his judgments,
>     and his paths beyond tracing out!
> "Who has known the mind of the Lord?
>     Or who has been his counselor?"
> "Who has ever given to God,
>     that God should repay them?"
> For from him and through him and for him are all things.
>     To him be the glory forever! Amen.

Paul is reminding us of God's credentials. Paul writes "in view of God's mercy." We don't just surrender because we are supposed to. We surrender in response to *His* overwhelming greatness and mercy.

Imagine that you have a serious heart issue. Your life depends on being sedated on a table in the operating room, your chest wall cut open by a surgeon—you're essentially surrendering to a surgeon's skill. I'm guessing you would do some research before making that decision. Would you rather surrender your outcome to someone who Googled how to do open-heart surgery, or a highly respected expert who graduated from a top-notch medical school? When your life is in the balance, credentials matter.

The bottom line is this: We will never surrender to a God we can't trust, and the only way to trust God is to know that He is good by personal experience. Paul's plea to us to sacrifice our lives and bodies to God depends on the assumption that we know our Lord.

## *KNOWING* JESUS CHANGES EVERYTHING

Unfortunately, in church culture we often talk about changing our behavior more than we encourage one another to know Jesus more deeply. Instead of seeing Jesus as someone to invite into your sexual questions and struggles, you probably feel like you have to get your act together. Maybe this is the first time that you've even considered that Jesus wants you to turn to Him with your doubts and pain.

Honestly, it might feel safer to just keep trying to fix things on your own rather than surrender. When we are trying hard, we still feel like we are in control. But surrender requires trust. The idea of surrendering your sexuality to Jesus might be absolutely terrifying. What might He ask you to change? Will He welcome you? Or will He reject you?

You won't surrender to someone you don't trust. And you can't trust someone you don't know. Most of us just don't know Jesus well enough to surrender an aspect of our life that is personal, vulnerable, and painful.

This is why it is *knowing* Jesus that changes everything. Knowing the Lord and surrendering to Him go hand in hand. The more you know Him, the more you will want to surrender. You will trust that His ways are better than yours and that He really will work out everything that happens for your good (Rom. 8:28). And the greater your surrender, the more you will experience intimacy with Him. This is the continuing journey that every Christian is called to be on. In reality, very few Christians have been discipled in the way of knowing Jesus.

There are a lot of very sincere Christians who live compartmentalized lives because they do not know how to surrender their sexuality to the Lord. Dan was one of them.

> When the church called me to serve as a pastor, I thought porn was in the past for me. It wasn't. In fact, the pressures of ministry only intensified the shame of my struggle. I'd often ask, "How can this still be in my life?"
>
> What I didn't realize was that my issue ran deeper than pursuing relief through porn. I hadn't fully grasped the heart of God. I was so focused on me: my failures, my perceptions, my performance in ministry, that I missed the God who says, "Come to me . . . for I am gentle and humble in heart" (Matt. 11:28–29). Intimacy with God was my issue. Over time, He would use His truth, fellow brothers and sisters in Christ, and compassionate counselors to drive me toward intimacy with the Savior. Surrendering to Him is now more of a privilege than a compulsion. Being with Him is a source of joy rather than deep shame. And pastoring is an opportunity to comfort others in the way He has comforted me in my struggle.

Elaine was another:

> I have spent most of my life believing that Christians should just "do" the right things and "obey" the rules. In the midst of my healing

> journey, these past few years I have come to understand that God wants to be with me. Like in the garden, He longs and desires to fellowship with me and He knows me intimately. He is not surprised by anything I have to say or anything I have done. I feel like I have come to personally understand and believe Ephesians 1:17–18, where it says that God will "give me the Spirit," that the "eyes of my heart may be enlightened." Surrendering my sexuality is an ongoing journey for me. It is a willingness to expose all of me to a holy God who is worthy of all my worship. It is an intentional yielding of my life and my sexuality to Him and the Spirit who dwells within me.

Both Dan and Elaine began by trying to get rid of sin and do all the right things in order to please God. But what eventually made the difference wasn't self-discipline, but cultivating true intimacy with God.

Most of us have only secondhand knowledge of what God says about us. We read it somewhere or hear it on a podcast or perhaps have a friend tell us about God's love. Frankly, that's not good enough. We have to know God for ourselves for His words to take root in our hearts.

***Surrender is not God's demand on your life, but rather His invitation to you. Surrender isn't ultimately about what we let go of, but about how much of God we are ready to embrace.***

Going to church or even reading your Bible doesn't change everything. You have to know the God whose name you carry. You can be a Christian for decades and never know Jesus in such a way that He makes a practical difference in your life. I know this because I lived this way for many years and even now can fall into the trap of trying to do life with very little of God.

Just yesterday, I felt overwhelmed by

some conflicts personally and in ministry. I had a two-hour drive all by myself and felt extremely anxious about what was before me. Trying to distract myself, I put on an audiobook, took a phone call, and then switched to some music. Then I remembered this message of surrender. So I prayed to God right there in my car, "Lord, I've been trying to do this in my own strength. I need to surrender these things to You and to know Your love, Your wisdom, and Your presence in the middle of it all."

Surrender is not God's demand on your life, but rather His invitation to you. He has promised every Christian the resurrection power of Christ Jesus in our lives. The result of His Spirit living in us is love, joy, peace, patience, kindness, goodness, faithfulness, gentleness, and self-control (Gal. 5:22–23).

Do you honestly have all of those things? Does your life speak of the power of God pouring in and through you?

The answer is probably no. We suppress the presence and power of the Holy Spirit because we want to stay in control. We don't know what it is to lay down our lives so that we can be filled with God's Spirit.

When we live our Christian life segmented, inviting God into some areas but not others, we will lack the passion, the power, and the transformation He promises. This is why it is critical for us to approach every area of life, including our sexuality, by inviting Jesus into it.

The message of "surrendered sexuality" is not meant to beat you over the head with shame in your sexual brokenness and struggles. Most likely, you know the "rules" about biblical sexuality, and you probably feel convicted by the ways you don't live up to them. But what you don't likely know (I didn't either!) is that God cares about far more than your sexual behavior.

As a Christian, surrender isn't ultimately about what we let go of, but about how much of God we are ready to embrace.

It is the choice and journey of laying it all down as Jesus modeled for us in His anguish as He faced the cross with the words, "Not my will, Father,

***Our surrender to God is both a onetime decision, and an ongoing battle to walk out that decision.***

but Yours be done in my life." Following His example, we surrender with a heart that says, "Jesus, I trust You to define what sex should be. I trust You to forgive and cleanse me. I trust You to make me whole in my brokenness. I trust Your goodness in what You both give and take away. I trust You with my past, my present, and my future."

Our surrender to God is both a onetime decision, and an ongoing battle to walk out that decision. During some seasons, our hearts are fully committed. And then just a short time later, we find ourselves discouraged or confused, trusting our own wisdom instead of surrendering to God's care.

We will talk a lot about sex in this book. I will share research, psychological principles, and some of my own thoughts. But on the journey of surrender we are going to return again and again to what it truly means to know Jesus and how that relationship informs everything about your sexuality—in singleness, dating, marriage, shame, sexual desire, forgiveness, love, loneliness—all of it!

As I've been on this journey in my own life, I've discovered the following things about the Lord.

### *In His love, God wants all of me*

I am so thankful that God relentlessly pursues every area of my heart! He is not content to have 90 percent of me. He redeemed all of me for all of Him. I gave my life to Christ almost five decades ago. Yet every year and through every season, I can see the Lord pursuing new territory in my heart, setting me free from my negative thoughts, my fears, my sin, and my shame.

God loves you way too much to ignore an area of your life that still looks like the "old you."

### *God is full of patience, mercy, and compassion*

While God desires all of me, He also is patient with the fact that surrender and trust involve a journey. Sometimes I wonder what it might be like if God let me see in one moment all that He wanted to claim within me. I'm so incredibly thankful that God is gracious and patient! God knows my limitations and that I would be destroyed by the knowledge of my sin and His holiness if I saw it all in one moment.

God invites you on a *progressive* journey of surrender. He will show you in each season by the searching of His Spirit what piece is for today. You are not supposed to read this book and be "fixed." This is just one step on your journey toward the Lord.

### *God's love is not dependent on my performance*

Like many who have been raised in Christian homes, I have linked my behavior with God's love. I have genuinely believed that if I did more good things and avoided sin, God would love me more. This has been a trap that has been very difficult for me to unlearn. Perhaps you can relate.

The enemy can take a message about surrendered sexuality and twist it to convince you that God's goodness and love are based on you changing your behavior. Please let this truth sink in: God does not and will not love you any more or less based on how well you follow the rules. It is God's love that will move you toward holiness, not your purity that moves God to love you!

### *God is good*

In my own journey of surrender, I have not wrestled much with what God's Word says, but I've wrestled to understand how a good God would say such things. I'm thankful to know that many who have gone before me, including godly people we read about in the Bible, have struggled to understand God's ways. The journey to know Jesus isn't about crafting a version of God that I can accept, but believing and pursuing the goodness of God as He is.

As you read this book, you will run into questions that I cannot answer. I cannot and will not try to explain to you how a good God would allow [you fill in the blank]. Some questions are bigger than an answer but require the very presence of God. I have wept with victims of human trafficking who have described evil beyond my imagination. And I have watched in awe as somehow, over time, the presence of God is a goodness far greater than any evil. While our unanswered questions may remain, they become mysteriously irrelevant when confronted by the lavish goodness of God.

Friend, in what ways do your doubts about sex, your shame, your disappointment, and your longings keep you from a deep, intimate relationship with God? What areas of your life do you feel like you must hide, minimize, or ignore when you step into church? What is the secret, relationship, fear, or habit keeping you from fully surrendering to the presence and power of God? God's love is greater than your doubts, your wounds, your shame, and your sin.

Take heart in this: Even as you strive to surrender, Jesus is pursuing you. He takes our meager cries for help and moves heaven and earth to meet us.

Remember my friend Shelly? She has been on a long journey of surrender. Here's how it began:

> Racked with pain and seeing no way out, I decided to take my life. Moments after saying out loud to myself "I can't do this anymore," the phone rang. An older woman from the church where I was married seventeen years earlier, the very same woman I would avoid in the grocery store, called out of the blue, extending an invitation to come to church. I heard God's voice in that call telling me to hold on. I asked Jesus, "If You're real, Jesus, show me."
>
> I went to church with this woman and on my way out grabbed the *Our Daily Bread* publication from the back table. The first devotion was in Romans 12:2. "And do not be conformed to this world, but

be transformed by the renewing of your mind, so that you may prove what the will of God is, that which is good and acceptable and perfect."

"God, what is Your good and acceptable and perfect will for me?" I begged Him.

I had a nice house with a manicured yard, a good husband who loved me, two beautiful children, a good job. From the outside looking in, I appeared to have it all, yet I was miserable and suicidal. Nothing satisfied the deep longing within me.

God reached down from heaven and humbled Himself to hear my cry for help. He loved me right where I was in the pit of depression and sin. He invited me to come to Him because I was burdened and heavy-laden so that He could give me rest. He told me to draw near to Him, that He was jealous for me and that without faith in Him, it was impossible to please God. He told me that *all* things work together for good for those who love Him and are called according to His purpose. He told me to believe that all things are possible. So I pursued a relationship with the living God and He loved me back to health. Although nothing outward had changed in my circumstances, He had given me a new heart and I was joyful inside!

I will be sixty this year. My experience with God hasn't been a sprint; it's a marathon. He saved me both from physical and spiritual death, and I have experienced nothing more satisfying than my relationship with Him. He is everything to me. I don't surrender perfectly, not by a long shot, but He is faithful and just and bears with me along the narrow path.

Like Shelly, tearing down the wall that separates you from God will require honesty, courage, and patience. We are going to look at your wall brick by brick and bring your thoughts and your questions before the supremacy and the power of the One who loves you and gave Himself for you (Gal. 2:20). We are going to look at the process of making that choice to surrender our sexuality to the Lord, but always and only in light of the journey of knowing Christ Jesus our Lord. Without an intimate relationship with God, the call to reorder your life (including your sexuality) will become a burden of legalism that you won't be able to handle for long.

Shelly's is a true story. Knowing Jesus really changes everything, and it can change everything for you. This book is about that process—the process of tearing down the wall between you and God so that He can give you life.

I am beyond excited to go on this journey with you. Why? Not because I hope God cleans up your sex life or changes your view on cultural issues, but because when God takes over that territory of your heart (the one behind the wall), you will experience a love, a power, and a freedom that defies explanation.

## Application Exercise:

---

In what ways have you separated your sexuality from your relationship with God? Honestly mark all that apply.

- ☐ I have a sin struggle that I haven't told anyone about.
- ☐ I question the goodness of what the Bible says about sex.
- ☐ I have sexual wounds that God hasn't healed or redeemed.
- ☐ My sexuality is a source of shame.
- ☐ I don't fully believe that I am forgiven and cleansed from past sexual sin.
- ☐ My sexual identity feels more real and powerful than what the Bible says about me.
- ☐ I don't feel comfortable praying about my sex life.
- ☐ What the Bible says about sex seems outdated and irrelevant.
- ☐ Other: ______________________________

Which of these areas of questions and pain are currently creating doubt or distance in your relationship with God?

- ☐ I can't understand why God allows things like sexual abuse or human trafficking.
- ☐ Experiences in the church that were hypocritical, judgmental, or abusive
- ☐ The way Christians argue about sexuality
- ☐ The silence in my church on important sexual issues
- ☐ The unloving stance some Christians have toward the LGBTQ+ community
- ☐ My own experience of God not delivering me from a sexual struggle
- ☐ Unresolved sexual conflict within my marriage
- ☐ Other: ______________________________

Talk to at least one Christian brother or sister this week about your answers to these questions. Ask for them to pray for you and with you as you engage in this study.

### Passages to Study:

---

***Read John 4:1–26.***

How did this woman possibly have her sexual brokenness "walled off" from her pursuit of God?

How did Jesus invite her to tear down that wall?

What happened as a result?

***Read Psalm 139.***

How does this psalm challenge your assumption that you can separate your sexuality from God's knowledge or presence?

What specific verses in this psalm encourage you to invite and acknowledge God's presence in the most intimate spaces of your life?

***Read Romans 11:33–12:2.***

Paraphrase what this passage means to you personally.

## Questions for personal reflection and discussion:

---

1. "Sexuality is never a neutral issue in your relationship with God." Do you agree with this statement? Why or why not?
2. Why is it a problem to ignore sexual issues, questions, and struggles?
3. How would you describe the difference between surrendering and trying harder?
4. How would you describe the extent to which you have surrendered your sexuality to the Lord?
5. Why do you think Christians tend to "compartmentalize" their sexuality rather than surrendering it to God?
6. Why is knowing Jesus so important to your journey of surrender?

CHAPTER 2

# Surrendered Identity

Think about this question: What is the most important thing about you? Out of all the things that define you, which is the most central?

As a Christian, you probably know what the *churchy* answer is: Jesus. But in reality, is Jesus a more powerful force in your identity than your loneliness? Your sexual desire? Your marital status? Your sexual history?

When we talk about sex in the church, we usually talk about how Jesus wants to change our behavior. He wants you to stop struggling and giving into sexual sin. Because of this, we may believe that we can change our identity by making different sexual choices. Maybe if we stop sinning, we can be a real Christian and truly experience God's love. But what if it's the other way around?

If you are a Christian, the most important passage in the Bible about your sexuality is this one: "Therefore, if anyone is in Christ, the new creation has come: The old has gone, the new is here!" (2 Cor. 5:17).

## WHAT IS IDENTITY?

Identity is incredibly complicated. You have so many things that make you, you. Your age, gender, physical appearance, ethnicity, and family history. Your talents and weaknesses, your successes and failures, your likes and dislikes. And throughout life, identity markers keep changing! Your beauty, marital status, reputation, and occupation can all change in a heartbeat, and they definitely evolve over time.

God does not call us to integrate a Christian identity with every other defining marker, but to identify with Him as our Creator, Redeemer, and Lord. Every other identity pales in comparison to the most important thing about me: I belong to the Lord. I am His.

We live in a day where people define themselves by their sexuality. Are you married, divorced, or single? Gay or straight? What are your personal pronouns? In church culture, we may subtly ask, "Are you sexually pure or broken?"

God wants you to know Him in such a way that all these things take a back seat to what He says about you. Being a Christian means that every other identity is secondary to the fact that your life is now "hidden with Christ in God" (Col. 3:3).

Your sexual struggles may be symptoms of a much deeper spiritual battle—the battle for your identity in Christ. You may have tried to not experience same-sex attraction. You may have sworn off dating apps. You may be fighting against the shame of your past sexual choices. You may be struggling and determined to stop giving in to sexual sin. But you can't break free. Why? Because your sexuality has become a defining factor of what it means to be "you."

**God doesn't change *what we do* until He first and foremost changes *who we are*.**

Every single one of us has an identity problem. And that identity problem will bleed into every other aspect of our lives, including sexuality. In this chapter, we are going to tackle a few identity traps—self-discovery, shame, performance, and relationship—and then look at how you can find freedom from these through knowing Jesus.

## THE SELF-DISCOVERY TRAP

What would you do if you went out for a hike and got lost? Let's say you had no cellphone coverage and no way of figuring out your way home. Most likely, you would depend on your memories ("I think we should go this way") and things around you ("This tree looks familiar"), and you might be right. But a far more reliable way to navigate your journey would be to trust something that doesn't change. The sun always rises in the east and sets in the west. Or an instrument like a compass that can orient you based on "true north." Even when it felt like you were going the wrong way, you could trust a source of reliable information.

Navigating your identity is much like this. Everyone feels lost at times, trying to figure out what is most important and most true about themselves. Instead of relying on trustworthy, unchangeable truth, we tend to rely on our feelings as our own internal compass.

This has increasingly become our strategy in a postmodern culture. Abigail Favale explains why: "Postmodernism, to put it simply, is the worldview that sees reality in terms of narratives that are created by human beings, rather than an order of objective truths that can be discovered by human beings."[1] In other words, you need to create your identity.

> ***Sex was once regarded as something human beings did. Today it is seen as vital to who human beings are.***

Postmodernism assumes that reality is not discovered externally, but created internally. The most trustworthy source of truth is your own feelings, experiences, and desires. Nothing is fixed or assumed, and you are the only one who can discover the "true you." As a result, sexual desire, sexual and gendered experiences, and romantic relationships have an outsized role in how you understand yourself. Carl Trueman, author of *Strange New World,* explains how "sexual desire has emerged in the last one hundred years as a primary category for understanding our identity. In biblical times or in ancient Greece, sex was regarded as something human beings *did*; today it is considered to be something vital to who human beings *are*."[2] We believe our identity is defined by who we are sexually.

Children at the youngest ages are encouraged to begin a self-discovery process in order to create a story of self. A friend recently told me that her daughter is the only girl in her sixth grade class who does not identify as gay or bisexual. These are girls who are eleven and twelve years old who have never had a sexual relationship, yet they see themselves as gay or bisexual due to the pressure to create a story of self based on feelings and cultural influence.

The impact of merging sexual desires with identity does not just play out with those who identify as LGBTQ+. It impacts all of us. When we buy into cultural thinking, we begin to believe that our desires define us, and we must act on what we desire to find fulfillment and to live authentically. It seems unthinkable, for example, to stay in an unfulfilling marriage or to say no to someone you are attracted to. This is why the biblical sexual ethic seems so offensive to our cultural norms. God is telling us not just to *stop doing* something, but to stop *being someone*—to deny your "authentic self," as the contemporary thinking goes.

The truth is, God never intended for you to create your own meaning by following your heart or giving in to your longings. This is not to minimize what you are experiencing. Feelings and desires can be powerful! And honestly, our longings at times can feel much more promising than our relationship with God.

Pastor Casey Shutt gives this illustration to help us understand how the trap of self-discovery eventually leads to feeling even more lost:

> Imagine a sailor, new to the ship and crew, confused as to where the ship is heading. It's nighttime, and the ship's movements don't square with his training to use the North Star as a fixed reference point. So the

confused sailor asks, "Captain, where are we going?"

The captain replies, "We do things a little differently here. See the lantern on the ship's bow? That's our guiding light. That's how we're making our way across the sea."

No wonder the ship's movements don't make sense. Guiding a ship by a reference point *on the ship* means the ship is adrift, voyaging to nowhere.

Human life is like a ship. To get where we're meant to go, we must have a reference point outside of both ourselves and our world. We need a North Star.[3]

Our desires and longings tell us something about what is happening inside us, but they are never a trustworthy guide for a fulfilling life. Instead, God tells us as His children to trust Him as the compass of our lives. "Your word is a lamp for my feet, a light on my path" (Ps. 119:105).

## THE SHAME TRAP

I have a young friend who recently went through a painful divorce. Through processing her grief, she said, "I never dreamed that I would wear the label of a divorced woman." Another friend struggling with the fallout of a wrong sexual choice said, "I never thought that I would belong in that category!"

You may not have said the words out loud, but I wonder if you have ever thought them. What label do you wear because of your sexual past or current struggle?

In a cruel twist, we determine our worthiness not only by what we have done sexually, but also by what has been done to us. Almost without exception, victims of sexual abuse believe they are to blame for the sin against them. Those who have suffered sexual trauma almost always battle a deep sense of unworthiness.

Your sexuality—your desires and your sexual history—all play a major role in whether you see yourself as a "good" person. This becomes increasingly true when you become a Christian and begin to realize some things you desire and some things you've done are defined by God as immoral and wrong. Jesus died to free us from the shame of our sin and struggles, but the enemy can ironically turn your experience of Christianity into the exact opposite. The "good news" of the gospel seems to turn into a huge burden of shame you just can't shake.

Sexual sin can feel more shameful than anything else we might struggle with or experience. In your small group, people may confess getting angry in traffic, caring too much about material things, or gossiping about a friend, but when was the last time someone got real about a sexual struggle?

Shame is one of our greatest barriers to knowing the freedom that Christ died to give us. Our sexual shame can make us more vulnerable to sexual temptation and sin. Research shows that unaddressed shame is correlated with increased porn use, avoiding sex in marriage, sexually acting out, secret sexual behavior, and a lack of intimacy in relationships.[4] Not only do we act out of the shame we see in ourselves, but our sinful sexual behaviors reinforce the belief that we can never be free from that shame. Shame and sin can feel like a vicious cycle you can't escape no matter how hard you might try. This happened to Kyle.

***Jesus died to erase the labels that keep us bound to our sin.***

Growing up in a chaotic home with little guidance from his parents, Kyle found porn when he was ten. In middle school, he began asking classmates to text him nudes and eventually started experimenting with hookups. In college, a friend invited Kyle to an event with the campus ministry Cru, where he gave his life to Jesus. He started reading the Bible, attending a discipleship group, and learned that many of the things he had done sexually were wrong. Kyle felt ashamed of his sexual history, so kept it a secret. He thought, *If my Christian friends knew what I've done, they would kick me out.*

Even as he grew in his relationship with God, Kyle continued to struggle with sexual sin, hooking up with women he met through dating apps. He rationalized, "I've already messed up. It's not like I can be a virgin again."

I love how Paul confronted this belief. He wrote to the Corinthian Christians, "Do you not know that wrongdoers will not inherit the kingdom of God?" Then Paul lists the sins of these wrongdoers. But, he assures Kyle and us just as he encouraged the Corinthians, "And that is what some of you *were*." But now, he reminds them, "you were washed, you were sanctified, you were justified in the name of the Lord Jesus Christ and by the Spirit of our God" (1 Cor. 6:9–11).

I imagine that some of the Christians Paul was writing to still struggled with sexual sin. They had memories and regrets from past experiences. But Paul told them plainly, "You *used to* define yourself with these labels. That's not who you are now!"

For many Christians, the label of "sexual sinner," "fallen leader," "adulterer," "sex addict," and "sex offender" is so powerful that it becomes a lifelong identity. Yes, there are earthly consequences for sin, but Jesus died to erase the labels that keep us bound to our sin.

Shaking shame is easier said than done.

One friend, who battled shame for many years, described what a wise friend said that finally freed her:

> After I began to have a personal relationship with Jesus, I continued to experience overwhelming shame for my sexual sin. I carried that shame until I met an older man full of wisdom who helped me understand that I didn't have to carry the burden of all my sin and shame.
>
> I pushed back on him about how he didn't understand how horribly I had sinned.

> As I cried, the man handed me a tissue and I blew my nose. He then pointed out that, just as I had to decide to accept the tissue, I also had to decide to receive God's forgiveness. I wouldn't hand a dirty Kleenex back to this kind man after I had used it and made it mine. Was I giving Christ's gift of forgiveness and cleansing back to Him or was I going to decide to believe that His death on the cross had cleansed me from all my sin and shame?
>
> This experience changed my life and I no longer carry with me the shame of the choices I made that brought me to despair.

The Bible says in 1 John 1:6–7, "If we claim to have fellowship with him and yet walk in the darkness, we lie and do not live out the truth. But if we walk in the light, as he is in the light, we have fellowship with one another, and the blood of Jesus, his Son, purifies us from all sin."

## THE PERFORMANCE TRAP

The shame trap has a close relative called the performance trap. It says in a nutshell: If you can lose your purity through sexual sin, that means you can also earn it through the right behavior.

I have struggled with the performance trap throughout my Christian life. I was the poster child for the good Christian kid. I'm embarrassed to say it, but I actually won awards at school for "Outstanding Christian" (whatever that means). I did all the right things and avoided obvious sins.

Getting applause from the Christian adults in my life, I concluded that I could earn God's love with the right behavior, including sexual behavior. In college, I was the kid giving talks on why you should save sex for marriage.

But my heart was rooted in pride and spiritual competition. I wanted to be a better Christian than my friends. And beneath all of that spiritual performance, I was terrified of messing up. If I could earn God's love with my behavior, that meant I could also lose it.

C. S. Lewis warned, "Whenever we find that our religious life is making us feel that we are good—above all, that we are better than someone else—I think we may be sure that we are being acted on, not by God, but by the devil . . . [The devil] is perfectly content to see you becoming chaste and brave and self-controlled provided, all the time, he is setting up in you the Dictatorship of Pride."[5]

***Jesus often talked about two different kinds of people who needed help: those in shame* and *those in self-righteousness.***

This described me.

Eventually, I met people with heart-wrenching stories of sexual abuse, sexual confusion, and seasons of sexual sin. These friends loved Jesus as much as I did, but their journey of surrender was marked with pain and shame. Rather than feeling proud because I had a cleaner history, I was humbled by their unfaltering determination to find freedom. Frankly, it cost them more to follow Jesus than it did me. They became people I looked up to instead of those I thought I was better than.

Jesus often talked about two different kinds of people who needed help: those in shame *and* those in self-righteousness. You might be familiar with the story of the prodigal son (see Luke 15), a story about a father and two brothers.

One brother wanted to do life his own way. He disregarded his father's love, took his inheritance while his father was still living (which would have been a huge disgrace in that time), went far away, and spent his money on partying and prostitutes. The other brother stayed home with his dad and did everything that was expected of him.

Eventually, the younger son came to his senses. Although desperate to come home, he felt too ashamed to be his father's son. He finally did, and was welcomed back by his father. But the older brother resented his brother and the father's warm welcome. "All these years I've worked hard and never disobeyed you," he told his father. He felt that he had earned his father's love while his younger brother had squandered it. Both brothers faced a barrier in their relationship with their father.

Jesus told this story to help us understand that both of these identities, shame and performance, will keep us from being surrendered to the Lord. Shame tells us that we can never be worthy; self-righteousness tells us that we have earned the love of God (and must keep earning it).

John Newton, the former slave trader who wrote the well-known hymn "Amazing Grace," had reached the end of his life. His final recorded words were, "My memory is nearly gone, but I remember two things; that I am a great sinner and that Christ is a great Savior."[6] Wholeness means holding these two truths in tension. The son who was covered in shame knew the bad news about his sin, but not the good news of his father's love. The brother who obeyed knew the father's love, but thought he earned and deserved it. He was blind to the poison of his sin.

Do you ever walk into a room and think, "If only they knew what I have done, they would want nothing to do with me"? Have you ever thought, "I believe God forgives me, but I will never be able to forgive myself"?

On the other hand, do you battle pride and self-righteousness, feeling confident that your sin is minor compared to your neighbor's?

The truth of our unworthiness and Jesus' righteousness that makes us worthy can heal both of these identity wounds.

## THE RELATIONSHIP TRAP

We don't have a sex problem. We have an intimacy problem.

I remember reading a book to my children when they were young called *Are You My Mother?*[7] A baby bird gets separated from his mother and approaches everything in sight asking the question, "Are you my mother?"

We don't know *who* we are until we know *whose* we are. Human beings were made to attach, to belong, and to bond.

God created us to be in families, to have committed and significant relationships, and to feel like we belong. Unfortunately, we live in a digital and mobile world in which the intimacy and belonging we so long for are sabotaged.

Our broken families and busy schedules have torn down a sense of heritage, unconditional belonging, and love. For example, approximately 25 percent of Americans are growing up without a father in their household.[8] The average American moves 11.7 times in their lifetime, disrupting long-term relationships and community.[9] Our most frequent relational interactions now happen digitally, keeping us from eye contact, physical touch, and the embodied presence of people who know us. Even if you grew up with your family physically around, you may have experienced attachment wounds causing you to feel isolated and lonely even when you are surrounded by people. Loneliness is now widely considered an epidemic, particularly in Western countries like America.[10] We can be constantly with people but still feel invisible.

Research consistently demonstrates a correlation between unhealthy family patterns and challenges with unwanted sexual desire and sexual dysfunction.

God created us for connecting: for intimacy and community. When we lack the healthy relationships that support our identity in Christ, we can end up looking to romantic and sexual relationships as the primary way we define ourselves.

When this happens, you can find yourself going from relationship to relationship. You may become enslaved by the pressure to have the perfect body. Or you might compromise your convictions and your body so that you can be "somebody's somebody." Even the experience of sex can feel like it at least temporarily helps you feel seen, loved, and connected to another person. Or perhaps you blur the lines of friendship and allow unhealthy codependent behavior so you can feel the intimacy of needing to be needed.

While God created you for relationship and connection, He never intended your identity to be dependent on your relational status, physical beauty, or sexual experiences. These are very unstable foundations on which to understand your value. Yes, we need encouragement, friendship, and connection with other people. But even our richest relationships can't be a substitute for God's love. God's words are eternal, and His love is truly unconditional and unshakable. Unhealthy relationships revolve around how people feel about you (which can quickly change). Healthy relationships reflect and remind you of who God is and what *He* says about you (which will never change).

Throughout the Bible, God describes His relationship with His people using the most intimate of terms and metaphors. He is your Father. You are His precious and loved child. He is your Beloved, your Husband. He is the Shepherd who calls you by name and saves you when you wander. He numbers the hairs on your head and provides for you. He knows every word before you speak it. He has promised to never leave you. He has given you His Spirit to literally live inside you. Like a vine is connected to a branch, you are to live in absolute dependence on Him.[11]

Think of every earthly experience of closeness, tenderness, intimacy, and love. Combine them all, and you may be getting close to the intimacy God created for us to have in Him.

If you are familiar with Paul's letter to the Ephesians, you know that he gets into how we are to act as Christians. (We will get there too in the following chapters.) But Paul understood that a changed life can only come from a true change in identity. You can't truly love God until you know how deeply He loves you. Read his prayer for the Ephesian church and let it also be for you:

> I pray that out of his glorious riches he may strengthen you with power through his Spirit in your inner being, so that Christ may dwell in your

> hearts through faith. And I pray that you, being rooted and established in love, may have power, together with all the Lord's holy people, to grasp how wide and long and high and deep is the love of Christ, and to know this love that surpasses knowledge. (Eph. 3:16–19)

When we experience this rich intimacy both with God and with His family, we can accept sex and marriage for the gifts they were meant to be, rather than as a solution for our loneliness or fear of rejection.

Are you beginning to see why identity is such an important part of surrendering your sexuality to God? Jesus doesn't just speak into your sex life. He has also profoundly spoken into your identity. He literally wants to transform how you understand what it means to be "you."

## LIVING IN YOUR NEW IDENTITY

Have you ever felt like these powerful truths of God are stuck in your head? You may have been told a thousand times that God loves you and that He sees you, but it doesn't make a bit of practical difference in how you navigate your journey of identity.

Seriously, what feels more powerful in how you see yourself—what God says or how other people treat you? Would you be more affected by the Bible passage you read this morning or by a friend who betrayed a confidence?

> ***Living in the identity Jesus died to give you is not based on a feeling, but based on a choice to believe something that doesn't always feel true.***

Surrendering your identity means that you believe what God says enough to actually start living your life based on it.

Several years ago, I had the chance to do a high ropes course. If you haven't seen one, it's basically an obstacle course about seventy-five feet in the air. You absolutely can't fall because they hook you into a secure harness with cables. While I knew this was true, I was still scared out of my mind to take a step on the balance beam six stories above the ground.

Trusting God with your identity might feel like this. Living in the identity Jesus died to give you is not based on a feeling, but based on a choice to believe in the security that you literally can't fall.

Your greatest problem is not your sexual temptations, your desires, or your wounds. Your greatest problem is that you don't believe the foundational truth of what God says about you.

You might be able to tell your neighbor with great conviction, "God loves you! He forgives you!" But you can't quite believe that enough to stake your own life on that truth.

What will give you the keys to living in the identity Jesus has given you?

Jim Wilder and Michael Hendricks wanted to understand why Christians have such a hard time living out the truth of what Jesus says about them. They wrote a book called *The Other Half of Church*, explaining how our brains have two sides (most people call it the right and left brain). The left side of our brain helps us process facts, logic, and problem-solving while the right side of the brain helps us form relationships and our identity.

Wilder and Hendricks found that most Christians try to change only by using the left brain. They read books and listen to sermons that give them information, but true transformation happens when we combine these truths with relational connections.

"The right brain processes these questions: Who is happy to see me here? What do I feel right now? Is there anyone here who understands me? How do I act like myself right now? What do my people do in this situation? The answers to these questions drive our character development."[12]

Wilder and Hendricks point out that we are neglecting important practices and relationships that help make God's truth become real in our lives. Most Christians, even if they know the Bible well, lack an intimate relationship with God, and their church-family relationships are superficial and short-lived.

Your identity in Christ is a fact, but you will fail to walk in it unless you reorder your life to connect meaningfully with both God and with other Christians. What you've read in this chapter and what you will read in the pages that follow will be only an intellectual exercise if you do not work out these truths spiritually and relationally. Here are a few ways you can begin to do this.

### *Establish the priority of knowing God*

At one stage of my life, I began to face some of the deep insecurities I had about my identity. I am a clinical psychologist and also tend to be introspective. Naturally, I spent time looking at my childhood, examining my thoughts, and trying to talk myself into believing what the Bible says about me.

My introspection helped me understand myself better. I was able to piece together early childhood experiences that fueled my compulsions and my fears of rejection. But insight alone couldn't transform me. It just helped me understand my brokenness. *I never found freedom by looking inward.*

> ***Things began to change as I shifted my focus to knowing God—not just knowing about Him, but knowing Him.***

Even reading the Bible wasn't enough. Biblical truth sometimes made me feel frustrated. I thought, "If I really am a new creation in Christ, why don't I feel like it? Why do insensitive words from a friend or a failure at work make me feel unlovable? And why am I so addicted to approval and success?" I knew I was in a trap, but I didn't know how to set myself free. I would obsess about what people thought of me, terrified of letting people down (and ultimately of letting God down).

Things began to change as I shifted my focus to knowing God—not just knowing about Him, but knowing Him. I needed to hear His voice and learn to, by faith, put weight on what He says about me. This has been a progressive journey, but it began about fifteen years ago with an intention to trust Jesus and fix my eyes on Him. I was in my early forties, in full-time Christian ministry, when I began to realize that I didn't really know Jesus. Yes, I trusted Him as my Savior, but I didn't know Him in such a way that it changed everything. Did Jesus love me personally? Did He really know my name?

One day, while thinking about God's call for us to love Him with all our heart, soul, and mind, I realized that I didn't know how to love God with my heart. My relationship with Him was built around head knowledge and trying to do all the right things, but my heart was distant from Him. Spending time with God felt like a box that I needed to check in order to please Him.

I wanted to love Jesus beyond just going through the motions. I began to start my day on my knees, asking God to show me His love and to draw me into actually knowing Him as Father, as Son, and as Holy Spirit.

I wonder if you've ever had the experience of being surrounded by the things of God but not walking intimately with Him.

Let me encourage you that God wants you to know Him. He is waiting for you to seek Him! God promises, "You will find me when you seek me with all your heart."

Do you long to know God like this? Do you want to know Him so intimately that you define yourself by who He is and who He says you are? If so, there are rhythms that can help you establish that kind of relationship with God.

Knowing God in this way begins with intention. I love David's cry in Psalm 63: "You, God, are my God, earnestly I seek you; I thirst for you, my whole being longs for you!"

This is not just a onetime prayer but a daily cry to return to.

You might start by setting aside twenty minutes either when you wake up or before you go to bed. (It can definitely be longer, but you might want to start with a time frame that isn't overwhelming.) Your time with God can include:

**Prayer.** A Pew research study found that 55 percent of Americans pray daily, making it the most common spiritual practice.[13] But many of us, if we are honest, have the same questions as the disciples who asked Jesus, "How should we pray?" Prayer is not just talking to God, but being with Him. It's a discipline we grow in as we take time to be quiet before God, to pour out our concerns, and to ask Him to lead us in the practical decisions and challenges of our daily lives.

**Bible reading.** God talks to us through the Scriptures. You might start by reading a chapter of the Bible every day. Take advantage of Bible study tools like the Bible Project and Bible reading plans like those provided by the YouVersion app. When you read the Bible, reflect on what you are learning about God and what God is showing you about yourself.

**Worship.** Many people think of worship as what you do on a Sunday morning. Yes, that is worship, but we develop intimacy with God through private worship. I want to see God, give my heart to Him, and reflect on His beauty and holiness. Often I play worship music that helps me focus on who God is and how much I love Him. Other ways to worship include speaking psalms of praise aloud; making a list of what you love about God; reading out loud the words of classic hymns; writing a poem or a letter about who God is and expressing your love for Him.

### *Find your Christian brothers and sisters*

When we look at how Jesus interacted with His disciples and how early church leaders like Paul and Peter encouraged the early Christians, they did more than preach sermons. They formed discipleship communities. The church was not just a place to hear a Sunday sermon, but a family that worshiped the living God, shared life, and challenged one another. Unfortunately, we've often made church into a superficial gathering rather than a family.

Your identity in Christ Jesus is not just a personal identity, but also a corporate identity. Most often, the Bible addresses us as a united group of believers, not as individuals. Yes, Jesus knows you by name, and you must have a personal relationship with Him one-on-one. But there's more to it than that. You won't be able to live in your true identity without understanding that you are part of something far greater.

In every community and city are other Christ followers who are your brothers and sisters. These are not just meant to be people you see at church on Sunday, but those who are called to be like your family, loving you with unconditional love, carrying your burdens, and helping you grow in your faith.

Your faith family probably won't seek you out. Rebecca McLaughlin advises, "Stop asking, 'Who will love me?' Instead ask, 'Who can I love?' . . . When we sit around and think, *Who will love me?* loneliness and discontent creep in. But when we give ourselves to loving people, we will find that love boomerangs back at us when we least expect it."[14]

Over the years, I've usually been the one to start small groups that go deeper than the average Christian gathering because *I desperately need these communities*! I've prayed for and searched for spiritual moms, dads, brothers, sisters, sons, and daughters because *I need them*!

Most churches offer some kind of small group program and will help those who want to start or lead a small group. While you don't have to do this alone, you may need to take the initiative. Finding your faith family is going to take time, intentionality, and vulnerability on your part. Don't wait for someone to come find you. Act by faith knowing that the Christians around you are just as desperate for this type of community as you are.

***Pursue discipleship***

Discipleship involves accepting the guidance of more mature Christians who can encourage you in your pursuit to know and follow Jesus. Discipleship is so important that Jesus sometimes said no to opportunities to reach large crowds, choosing to invest in a small group of committed followers.

Discipleship can happen one-on-one, but is particularly powerful when small groups of believers commit to learning together. It's more than just meeting to share concerns and prayer requests, but intentionally committing to the practices and vulnerability that will foster long-term growth. Healthy Christian churches always offer a path of discipleship. Ask about it! If your church doesn't have a discipleship path, find a mature Christian around you and ask him or her to disciple you.

You might not find that these practices make a difference right away, but if you commit to it, God's voice will become more powerful in your life.

✦ ✦ ✦

Friend, be aware of how your identity trap flavors how you read the rest of this book. Remember the most important thing that God has to say about your sexuality: "If anyone is in Christ, the new creation has come: The old has gone, the new is here!"

Learning to truly believe and walk in this new identity is a lifelong process. I still have seasons where I struggle with doubt, shame, self-righteousness, and putting too much importance on what other people think about me. But with practice, I am learning what it is to look at the unchanging truths of my Lord and His promises. This helps me find my footing when the rest of my world seems to be swirling.

We have many things we use to define ourselves. All of those labels and descriptions need to come under the love and authority of what God has spoken to be true.

**You are not** your wounds.

"By his wounds we are healed."—Isaiah 53:5

**You are not** your sin.

"God made him who had no sin to be sin for us, so that in him we might become the righteousness of God."—2 Corinthians 5:21

**You are not** your shame.

"There is now no condemnation for those who are in Christ Jesus."—Romans 8:1

**You are not** your sexual desires.

"Do not live the rest of [your] earthly lives for evil human desires, but rather for the will of God."—1 Peter 4:2.

**You are not** your purity.

"While we were still sinners, Christ died for us."—Romans 5:8

**You are not** your relational status.

"The Spirit himself testifies with our spirit that we are God's children."—Romans 8:16

## Application Exercise:

---

This chapter addressed four common identity traps related to sexuality. Which of these four is most true of your journey?

- ☐ The Self-Discovery Trap
- ☐ The Shame Trap
- ☐ The Performance Trap
- ☐ The Relationship Trap

How does that particular identity issue play into your current questions or struggles related to sexuality?

Write down at least one or two core lies you tend to believe about your identity. Some examples might include:

No one would ever love me if they knew my struggle.
I need to be married to feel like a whole person.
I have to give a dating partner sex if I want them to love me.
My same-sex desire is a core part of my identity.
I only have value and worth if someone finds me worth pursuing.
I am still a virgin, so I'm a righteous person.

When did you first start believing that lie?

How, based on the Scripture, do you know it's a lie?

What is the truth?

What influences in your life reinforce the lie?

What influences in your life reinforce the truth?

Identify at least one person currently in your life who can walk this journey toward truth with you.

## Passages to Study:

---

***Read Philippians 3:4–11 and 1 Timothy 1:15.***

What words does Paul use to describe his identity apart from Jesus?

What happened for Paul to consider every other identity as "garbage"? See Philippians 3:8.

What do you think Paul means by the "surpassing worth of knowing Christ Jesus my Lord"?

To what extent have you experienced this?

***Read Ephesians 1–2.***

What truths about your identity do you find in these two chapters?

## Questions for personal reflection and discussion:

1. Do you believe that behavior shapes identity or identity shapes behavior? Explain your answer.

2. How has the postmodern pressure to write your own truth impacted your personal walk with the Lord?

3. What is the greater struggle for you: the shame of sexual sin or self-righteousness toward God and others? How are both of these barriers to surrender?

4. How would you describe the difference between the need for sex and the need for intimacy?

5. Why is knowing the Bible not enough to convince you of your identity in Christ?

6. What might it look like for you to pursue the deeper intimacy with God described in this chapter?

7. To what extent does your Christian community help you walk in God's truth about you? How can you take the initiative to find those types of relationships?

CHAPTER 3

# Surrendered Thinking

Picture a ten-year-old child who loves eating junk food. If he had his way, he would live on a diet of donuts, soda, candy, chips, pizza, and hot dogs. He gets incredibly annoyed when his parents keep these snacks out of the house and instead give him fresh fruits and vegetables, whole-grain bread, and grilled fish.

What if this kid never learned about nutrition? What if he grew up believing that all foods are equally nutritious? He would likely believe that his parents were either cruel or backward for denying him the food that he most desired.

## SURRENDER AND TRANSFORMED THINKING

Unfortunately, the average Christian is a lot like this in regard to sexuality. We know the rules about biblical sexuality, but have been trained to *think* like the world as a reference point of what brings wholeness and human flourishing.

Surrendering your sexuality to God can be a very painful process that means denying yourself pleasures and relationships that seem to be life-giving. If you only know the rules and never learned God's purpose, you will likely view God as either unloving or arbitrary.

Let's return to the passage about surrender from chapter 1: "Therefore, I urge you, brothers and sisters, in view of God's mercy, to offer your bodies as a living sacrifice, holy and pleasing to God—this is your true and proper worship. Do not conform to the pattern of this world, but be transformed by the renewing of your mind" (Rom. 12:1–2).

The ongoing process of surrendering ourselves to the Lord will always and must involve the ongoing process of thinking differently than the world does.

Before we even get to what it looks like to surrender your sexual sin and behavior to God, we need to address the importance of surrendering your thinking.

Christians tend to spend a lot of time discussing questions of *what*—what actions are sinful and acceptable—but neglect the more important questions of *why*. Why does God care so much about sex? Why shouldn't a person be able to engage sexually with the person they desire to? Why does sexual sin feel so much heavier than other sin struggles?

***We are creatures who will flourish as we embrace and live by the purpose of our Creator.***

We each believe a story about sexuality that helps us understand why we are sexual, what wholeness looks like, and why sexuality matters. Our world does not just have a different sexual ethic, but also operates with a different story of sex. The vast majority of Christians in the Western world have been unknowingly indoctrinated with the world's story of sex. When you believe the world's story of sex and then slap on God's rules, He will seem confusing at best. As Paul wrote, surrender must involve renewing our minds.

The topic of sexuality is a complex one, but at its core, your story of sex is rooted in the belief that *we are either creators or creatures*. The world believes we are our own creators with the authority to determine the purpose of our lives. The Bible tells a different story, that we are creatures who will flourish as we embrace and live by the purpose of our Creator. Creators *create* purpose; creatures *uncover* purpose.

## "YOU ARE THE CREATOR" ORIGIN STORY

A postmodern worldview puts you in the position of being your own creator. Based on the assumption that there are no absolute truths or purposes to discover, you get to create a story to make sense of your world.

Over time, we create both collective cultural stories and individual narratives that greatly influence how we think about our sexual and relationship choices. Our stories often operate at a subconscious level, which has an impact on our reasoning. Most of the time, we don't realize that we have ingested a cultural framework. Here are a few examples:

Within the last decade, our Western culture has created a new way to think about *male* and *female*. Gender is no longer viewed as the same thing as biological sex, but a separate sense of self that may be or may not be consistent with our physical bodies. We have also shifted to a belief that sexual preferences and desires are a core aspect of a person's identity.

You may not realize just how new it is for us to be thinking of identity in terms of sexual desires and our internal experience of gender. The words homosexual, bisexual, and heterosexual were only coined around 150 years ago. Although these sexual behaviors and desires existed, until recently they were not used to describe a person's identity. In a similar way, the word "transgender" was first used in the 1960s. Just a few decades ago, the idea of many different genders would have been rejected within American culture. Now, it has become a standard assumption in our educational, medical, and psychological systems.

We have also crafted a new way of thinking about marriage. Over the past fifty years, marriage has become more about "finding your soulmate" and falling in love than a basic societal institution built on commitment and family. Brad Wilcox, a sociologist who has been studying marriage for decades, explained what he calls the myth of the soulmate, "the idea that marriage is primarily about feeling an intensely emotional or romantic connection with 'the one' that makes you happy and fulfilled. This is a model of marriage deeply shaped by the expressive individualism that took off in the 1970s."[1] According to Wilcox, this has become the primary way to view marriage for most Western young adults. This idea is so pervasive that you might not even be aware of the fact that we didn't always think about marriage this way!

***Our culture falsely says you can only find happiness and wholeness by discovering (and in a sense, worshiping) your own desires.***

These shifts in our collective thinking didn't just happen but flow out of the foundational belief that *your sexuality reveals something about* ***you***. It tells the story of your internal sense of being—of your authentic self. You can only find happiness and wholeness by discovering (and in a sense, worshiping) your own desires. Everything from your sexual orientation to the choice to marry is tied to living from your heart and pursuing your true self. The burden is on you to discover and live your "best life."

From this thinking, we get the crises of "Did I marry the wrong person?" "How do I know if I am sexually compatible if we don't live together?" and "How could a loving God create me with sexual desires that I can't act on?"

This story of sex has influenced us far more than we realize. We have been repeatedly bombarded with assumptions that shape how we think about our sexuality. Assumptions like:

You must follow your romantic and sexual desires to find happiness.
Love is primarily a feeling. It's not an action or choice.
You should get married only if you are sexually attracted to and fall in love with someone who is your "soulmate."
Sexual activity is mostly for personal satisfaction and self-expression. If sex happens to involve marriage or having children by your personal choice, great, but the purpose of sex has little or nothing to do with marriage and procreation.
Gender is a social construct or internal understanding of self that may or may not line up with your biological sex.

If you look at God's rules for sex while still believing the culture's story of sex, you will view God as unloving, unreasonable, and insensitive to your needs and longings. Maybe you have felt this way. You can't understand why a good God would put restrictions on sexuality that limit your personal freedom and sexual expression. This is because you may be surrendering your *actions* to God while still holding on to a worldly and humanistic way of *thinking* about sexuality. You are looking for romance and sex to fulfill you, and you believe a good God should give you these things. This is, for many of us, the root of the barrier between us and God related to our sexuality. We have grown up in a culture that consistently tells us that we should create our own happiness and fulfillment.

Postmodernism is a form of idolatry, because it puts humans in the place of God. While viewing yourself as the creator may sound like freedom, every indicator of mental health and perceived happiness tells us that we are headed in the wrong direction. It should make us happier to live from our "authentic selves" but instead depression, anxiety, loneliness, and alienation continue to steadily increase.[2] We were never meant to carry the burden of being our own creators. In reality, our sexual feelings and desires are a fragile foundation on which to build a life.

## "YOU ARE THE CREATURE" ORIGIN STORY

The Bible shows us a very different way to think about our feelings, desires, and the purpose of sexuality. Instead of self-discovery, the purpose of our sexuality is God-discovery.

The Bible tells us that all of creation *reveals* the glory of God (Ps. 19:1) and that God reveals Himself through His creation (Rom. 1:20). God created for the purpose of revealing. Nothing in our physical or relational world is random, but created by a Designer with the intention of showing us who He is.

The Bible constantly refers to physical things and experiences that help us understand divine truths. Wolves and sheep, vines and branches, hunger and thirst, kings and servants. These are just a few physical pictures (or metaphors) within creation that teach us about spiritual truths.

Within our human experience, God has given us two powerful pictures to help us understand how He loves us. The first picture is fatherhood. When God says that He is your Father, what does that mean? In the last chapter, I referenced Jesus' story of the two brothers—the one who left home, spending his inheritance on sinful living, and the son who stayed home. This story is often referred to as being about the sinful son, but it is really a story about the father. In telling this story, Jesus' intention was for us to understand the heart of God, our Father, whose grace covers our sin and shame.

Our earthly experience of a father teaches us something about God. Even if you didn't have a good father, you have a sense of what a father should do. Good fathers love, discipline, and provide for their children. We look to our father for approval (and can spend a lifetime searching for the approval he never gave us). All those experiences of earthly fatherhood, for better or worse, affect your understanding of God's character.

The second picture God created to help us understand His love involves marriage and sexuality. Even reading this may creep you out. We don't usually talk about sex within the context of knowing God's love.

Let's spend some time unpacking this.

> ***Through our sexuality, God is revealing that God loves us not with romantic love, but with covenant love.***

The Bible is essentially a story of a wedding. In Genesis 2, before sin ever entered the world, we see Adam and Eve in the garden of Eden, enjoying intimacy with God. Then we read this: "That is why a man leaves his father and mother and is united to his wife, and they become one flesh" (Gen. 2:24). This verse refers to Adam and Eve, "naked and unashamed," but also the pattern of a man and a woman joining in the one-flesh relationship of marriage.

Fast-forward to the very end of the Bible and we see the prophecy of another wedding, but this one is between Christ and His bride, the church. John writes:

> "Let us rejoice and be glad
> and give him glory!
> For the wedding of the Lamb has come,
> and his bride has made herself ready." (Rev. 19:7)

The apostle Paul helps us understand that these two weddings are connected. He writes, quoting Genesis:

> "For this reason a man will leave his father and mother and be united to his wife, and the two will become one flesh." This is a profound mystery—but I am talking about Christ and the church. (Eph. 5:31–32)

This one statement from Paul pulls together the story of the Bible. The physical picture of love, intimacy, passion, and marriage is a literal illustration of the love that God has for His covenant people. God created male and female, sexual desires, longings, and experiences that all help us understand who He is and how He loves.

Through our sexuality, God is revealing that God loves us not with romantic love, but with covenant love.

## UNDERSTANDING COVENANT LOVE

Outside of the legal or theological world, you don't often hear the word "covenant." But you cannot fully understand God's purpose for your sexuality until you understand what covenant love means.

Tim Keller defined covenant this way: "A covenant relationship is a stunning blend of both law and love. . . . It is a relationship that is far more intimate and personal than a merely legal business relationship. Yet at the same time, it is far more durable, binding, and unconditional than one based on mere feeling and affection."[3]

When the Bible talks about God's love for you, it's not referring to a feeling, but to a deep, unchanging affection that has the full weight of His character behind it. While God loves all people as His creation, He does not extend this covenant love to everyone, only to those who have been chosen to be "His people." In the Old Testament, God's covenant people included the nation of Israel and foreigners who chose to join Israel in worshiping the Lord. Jesus came to usher in a new covenant—the covenant of His blood. Through Jesus' sacrifice on the cross, all people are now invited to become God's covenant people by believing in Him, but not all will choose Him.

Both God's covenant with Israel and His covenant with the church are described in the Bible using marriage and sexual language. Since we are New Testament Christians, you are probably familiar with the verses that say we are the bride of Christ. Here are a few Bible passages that use this word picture:

- Jesus told a story of ten virgins who were waiting for the bridegroom to come, referring to the importance of His church being prepared for His second coming (Matt. 25:1–13).
- Paul taught the early church that the marriage covenant, including the specific nature of a husband and wife, paint the picture of Christ's love for the church (Eph. 5:22–32).
- Paul responded to the Corinthian church's wandering with these words: "I am jealous for you with a godly jealousy. I promised you to one husband, to Christ, so that I might present you as a pure virgin to him" (2 Cor. 11:2).

While some of the imagery is lost on us because it refers to Jewish customs for betrothal and weddings, you can still see the main theme. I love the way author and teacher Christopher West brings this all together, making the connection between the wedding of Adam and Eve in Genesis, and the wedding of Christ and the church:

> Christ, the new Adam, "left" his Father in heaven. He also left the home of his mother on earth. Why? To give up his body for his bride (the church) so that she might enter into holy communion with him.[4]

The Old Testament is even more specific and graphic in describing God's covenant in marriage and sexual terms. For example, the entire prophetic book of Hosea is about a husband's faithful love to his wife, a prostitute, who keeps leaving him. This prophet's life was directed by God to be a picture of His covenant love with Israel and her unfaithfulness (Hos. 1:2; 3:1).

Here's the takeaway: God intentionally designed marriage, sexuality, and gender to be an earthly picture or metaphor that reveals the nature of God's covenant love.

## HOW COVENANT GIVES PURPOSE TO SEXUALITY

So how does understanding God's covenant love help you navigate sexual issues? Maybe you see the connection between God's love and *marriage,* but perhaps the application to sexuality feels like a bit of a stretch. You might have been attending church for decades without ever hearing this application.

It is critical for us to understand that God did not create sex primarily for marriage, but so that we might have an earthly illustration of His covenant love. You will not understand God's purpose for sex if you don't understand His design for marriage.

You don't have to *be* married to understand God's covenant love, but learning to appreciate biblical marriage will help you understand how God's design for sex and covenant reveals His covenant love. Let's take the example of adoption. Paul writes that we have been adopted into God's family.[5] You don't have to be adopted to grasp the beauty of being chosen by parents who are not your biological mom or dad, but you must understand what adoption actually is for the metaphor to mean anything to you.

So if you understand the example of God adopting us without having to be adopted yourself, you can understand how God reveals His love through the metaphor and sex and marriage even if you're not married. Sam Allberry, a pastor who has never married, explains, "If marriage shows us the shape of the gospel, singleness shows us its sufficiency."[6] Marriage is a temporary, earthbound picture of a far more important truth—the truth is that we were each made for an eternal, intimate covenant with God through Jesus Christ.

Unfortunately, many Christian singles have heard that "don't have sex" means "don't be a sexual person." You can't stop being a sexual person! In a similar way, you don't magically become a sexual person when you get married. You don't become a sexual person when you have sex. We were all created as gendered, sexual beings. God created you with sexual organs and hormones, along with longings for sex and romance. Your sexual longings and desires are meant to have an eternal echo of the call to be in covenant with God.

No matter where you go, you carry with you your social sexuality, being a relational, gendered person who needs intimate connection with others. As a Christian, you are called to be a spiritual mother or father, brother or sister, and son or daughter within the family of God. You also carry with you the capacity for erotic sexuality (the longings, desires, and potential of sexual acts that are meant to be exclusive to the marriage covenant).[7] Both married and single Christians are called not to deny but to steward their sexuality in light of the Creator's purpose and design.

The *purpose* of your sexuality and your gender is the same whether you are single, married, divorced, or widowed—to reveal God. Everyone experiences this metaphor of God's covenant love but from different perspectives, whether you are a single Christian, a Christian in a flourishing, life-giving marriage, or a Christian who has experienced the devastation of broken covenant and betrayal. (We will address this application to singles more completely in chapter 6.)

### *You were created for intimacy*

You are a sexual person because in your body, God has put the message of covenant love. You have longings and desires that make you feel empty without deep commitment and intimacy. Whether or not you get married, your sexual desire reminds you that you were not made to go through life alone. You need companionship, vulnerability, and intimacy. (Notice that I did not say you need sex.) Sexual desire is the physical prompt to pursue something greater than just having sex. Your experience of sexual desires and longings are not fulfilled in having sex, but in seeking the richness of covenant and intimacy. Our sexual longings remind us of the importance of intimacy and human connection God has made us for, but ultimately this physical longing points to a much deeper spiritual longing that reminds us to seek a relationship with the one true God. One based on covenant love which will never betray, change, or fade.

Are you really fulfilled through masturbation? Looking at porn? Hooking up? While these may give you an immediate release of sexual pleasure, they fail to satisfy you because you were created for more. Your sexual desire reminds you that you were made for intimacy—not a fleeting one-night stand, but to be known, loved and accepted, naked and unashamed.

### *The act of sexual intimacy is a bodily, sacred symbol of the covenant promise of marriage*

Why do Christians take Communion? Why do they get baptized? These are two specific, sacred things we do with our physical bodies to symbolize the spiritual covenant we have with God through Jesus Christ. With both baptism and Communion, doing the physical act without the spiritual commitment to God is empty because it misuses something that God has made sacred.

It may be helpful to think of sexual intimacy in this way. With sex, God has created our bodies to physically become "one flesh" in a way that symbolizes the choice we make in marriage to merge our lives together. Tim Keller explains:

> In a covenant, when you have made a promise, sex becomes like a sacrament. . . . Sacrament is an external, visible sign of an invisible reality. It's a symbol, an external symbol of an invisible reality. That's why it's so meaningful. When you use sex inside a covenant, it becomes a vehicle for engaging the whole person in an act of self-giving and self-commitment. . . . Sex is supposed to be a sign of what you have done with your whole life. . . . If you have sex inside a covenant then the sex becomes a covenant renewal ceremony. . . . In marriage when you're having sex, you're really saying, "I belong completely and exclusively to you and I'm acting it out"—that's what sex is. "I'm giving you my body as

a token of how I've given you my life. I'm opening to you physically as a token of the fact that I've opened to you in every other way."[8]

This is why God says that sex outside of marriage (even if you are deeply in love with a person) is sinful, while sexual intimacy within marriage (even when you don't feel so in love) is a meaningful and right pursuit. Sex is all about remembering the choice you made to covenant. These restrictions are not random or old fashioned but rooted in the Creator's purpose for our sexuality.

***The integrity of sexual faithfulness keeps the covenant intact***

God designed marriage to be based on the lifelong promise of faithfulness. Forsaking all others, till death do us part. You are making the decision to love even when you don't feel in love. Without such promises, you have a romantic relationship that will erode as soon as marriage becomes inconvenient or difficult.

I find it fascinating that almost 90 percent of Americans believe that it is morally wrong to cheat on your spouse. This means that many people who have no issue with premarital sex, pornography use, or threesomes hold the line on infidelity.[9] Perhaps this is because covenant is written in our hearts. We intuitively know that you don't have to get married, but if you do, you should keep your promise of sexual faithfulness.

Earthly marriage points to the importance of faithfulness in God's covenant with us. God's Word, His character, and His promises are why we can have a relationship with Him. Without this, we have no hope. God's words to His people include promises of His faithfulness like:

I will be your God and you will be my people (Ezek. 36:28).

I will never leave you nor forsake you (Deut. 31:8).

Nothing can separate you from the love of God in Jesus Christ (Rom. 8:38–39).

These promises are very similar to the vows a married couple makes. God wants us to look at the beauty and joy of a faithful, intimate marriage to understand His love for us. But He also wants us to look at the earthly picture of infidelity and realize the danger of being unfaithful to Him.

Maybe you have experienced the fallout of infidelity or betrayal in your own relationship or in your parents' marriage. If so, you understand the shock waves of pain and loss that come from breaking the marriage vow. Just as infidelity destroys the relationship of husband and wife, idolatry violates our covenant with God.

***Marriage and sex were created to be life-giving***

How did we get so far away from God's design for sexuality? Some people point to the invention of the internet, social media, pornography, or the iPhone as the factors that have caused such a domino effect. While many things have contributed, some believe that our view of sex and gender dramatically changed in the 1960s with the birth control pill. Abigail Favale explains the shift that occurred with birth control and the legalization of abortion: "We now think of sex as a *recreational*, rather than a *procreational*, activity. The connection between sex and the possibility of new life has been severed. . . . Pregnancy is often seen as a sexual mishap, a case of sex-gone-wrong, rather than the very outcome that sexual intercourse is designed to bring about."[10]

God's design for sex is procreative—that every sexual encounter has the capacity for new life. Not every married couple will have physical children; infertility is a deep, deep wound for many couples. Yet God designed marriage so that the intimacy of marriage should always generate life, sometimes physical life, but always spiritual and relational life. My husband, Mike, and I are way past childbearing, but the intimacy and love of our marriage overflows to our family and our community.

The same is true of our covenant with the Lord. How did Jesus tell us to know the genuineness of faith? By our fruit. The time we spend worshiping Him and knowing Him is the source of life in all we do. It is impossible for a deeply intimate life with God to be "fruitless," yet apart from that intimacy with Him, our works do not have spiritual life or power.

### *Male and female are part of the picture of covenant*

Many Christians will agree that marriage and covenant matter but wonder why such committed sexual love should be exclusively between a male and female. Or they are perhaps unsure that God has anything to say in response to questions about gender fluidity or being born in the wrong body.

> ***Male and female is not based on stereotypes or even roles that we play, but expressions of the personhood of God and the mystery of unity and uniqueness.***

We never see an example in the Bible of someone in a gay marriage or confused by gender, as we might understand it in our current day and age. Why is this? Not because we have been enlightened as human beings and now have a greater understanding of what it means to flourish in love and identity. We have these new questions because of the "humans are the creator" origin story.

While God never specifically answered all LGBTQ+ questions, He has very clearly established His design and purpose for male and female. The religious leaders were peppering and challenging Jesus with their "hot topics" of the day. In Matthew 19, they were specifically asking Him to settle an internal argument they had about divorce. Jesus answered the question by referring back to the Creator's words in Genesis:

> "Haven't you read," he replied, "that at the beginning the Creator 'made them male and female,' and said, 'For this reason a man will leave his father and mother and be united to his wife, and the two will become one flesh'?" (Matt. 19:4–5)

Jesus' words establish the importance of male and female and the gender-specific nature of marriage. Notice all of the gendered words He used in that short statement: male, female, man, father, mother, wife. Through this statement, Jesus reminds us of God's intent for marriage throughout all generations.

Male and female is not based on stereotypes or even roles that we play, but expressions of the personhood of God and the mystery of unity and uniqueness. We learn in Genesis that God expressed His image by creating two genders of humans—male and female (Gen. 1:27). The picture of the gospel involves the diversity of male and female becoming one flesh. They physically fit together; only the male and female intimate union can result in life. With all our technological advancements, we can only manipulate the materials that God has designed for us to carry within our bodies, but we cannot create a new design. We cannot make a man a woman or a woman a man, nor can we create life apart from an egg and a sperm.

I remember when I first heard this idea of God's story of sex explained to me. In all honesty, I walked right past it. It just didn't connect with me. It took me about five years to truly understand the significance of what God reveals about Himself through our gender and sexuality (and I'm still learning!). Understanding *why* God created us as male and female, *why* He created sex the way He did, and *why* He cares about our sexuality has greatly helped me connect with God's love and redemption. If you feel confused or overwhelmed by this concept, hang in there! We will refer back to God's story of sex throughout this book, but I want to contrast the basic assumptions between these two origin stories:

| We Are Creators: | We Are Creatures: |
|---|---|
| You must follow your romantic and sexual desires to find happiness. | What we choose is more important than what we feel. Sexual attractions and desires may come and go, but they don't define us or bring us long-term happiness. |
| Love is primarily a feeling that you cannot change. It's not an action or choice. | Covenant love is a decision, not a feeling. Within covenant, you work on sexual chemistry, feelings of love, and friendship. |
| You should get married only if you are sexually attracted to and fall in love with someone. | Getting married is a choice to honor God by living out the picture of the marriage covenant and family. Falling in love and sexual attraction are not wrong but are not the foundation of a godly marriage. |
| Sexual activity is mostly for personal satisfaction and self-expression. If sex happens to involve marriage or having children by your personal choice, great, but the purpose of sex has little or nothing to do with marriage and procreation. | Sexual activity is a unique way to remember and celebrate covenant and to create new life. |
| Gender is a social construct or internal understanding of self that may or may not line up with your biological sex. | Male and female are the only two categories of biological sex and gender. They were created to uniquely reflect God's nature and are not interchangeable in personhood or the covenant of marriage. |

## SPIRITUAL ATTACKS ON SEXUALITY, GENDER, AND MARRIAGE

How did you respond to reading about God's creation of sexuality? You might have been encouraged to learn that God has a story about your sexuality, or perhaps even the idea that God reveals His love through sexuality seems worlds away from your own experience.

Most, if not all, of us have experienced wounding, brokenness, and struggles that cloud our view of God's goodness in the gift of sex. There is a reason for this. If gender, sex, and marriage reveal God's love to us, then Satan works constantly to dismantle and distort what sex is supposed to reveal. What is under greater attack in our culture than sexuality, gender, and the covenant of marriage? Just think about how each of the following tear apart and tarnish the good gifts God has created:

Abortion
Sexual exploitation and human trafficking
Rape and incest
Pornography and sexting
Cohabitation
Domestic violence and abuse
Polyamory
Gender confusion
Hostility between male and female

The spiritual battle around sex is not just "out there" in the world and the media. It also is very real within your own heart, whether or not you recognize it. Without question, your experience of sex in some ways has been impacted by the spiritual battle both around you and within you.

Here are at least a few of the ways that likely has happened:

1. You have a distorted view of sex because you have been sexually used or objectified. Sex seems gross and unloving, and certainly not like a sacred gift from God.

2. You have been deceived about what is life-giving. You doubt God's goodness if He tells people not to have sex outside marriage and if He defines marriage as a lifelong commitment between one man and one woman. Maybe you obey out of obligation, but you cannot understand how those principles actually lead to greater human flourishing.

3. Whether married or single, you live with a love-hate relationship with marriage. It has become both the fairy-tale promise to meet your deepest longings and the greatest source of disappointment and rejection. One day you idolize it, the next day you are angry because of how it has failed to deliver.

4. Sexual issues, experiences, and questions have created distance between you and God. You are not sure if you can trust God, that He cares for you, or that He sees your pain.

5. Sexual shame is disqualifying you from the fullness of your calling. By God's grace, you might squeak your way into heaven, but covered with shame. You hide in the shadows of the church, you pretend to be someone you are not, and you squelch your calling to be a surrendered vessel in the mighty hands of God.

Take a moment to reflect. Which of these things is or has been true in your life? Have you ever recognized that this is a spiritual battle? Yes, it's playing out on the massive landscape of our culture, but it is just as consequential in your own soul.

We all live in a spiritual battlefield between the Creator's good purposes and an evil one who wants to destroy. And the stakes couldn't be higher. Christopher West explains:

> If the body and sex are meant to proclaim our union with God, and if there's an enemy who wants to separate us from God, what do you think he's going to attack? If we want to know what's most sacred in this world, all we need do is look for what is most violently profaned. The enemy is no dummy. He knows that the body and sex are meant to proclaim the divine mystery. And from his perspective, *this proclamation must be stifled*. Men and women *must be kept from recognizing the mystery of God in their bodies*.[11]

The message of the gospel is one of redemption. The Lord is not only our Creator, but also our Savior and Redeemer. Yes, Jesus died so that you can be with God forever. But the freedom and life that He gives should also give direction to your life on earth.

***God wants to not just fix our behaviors but transform our thinking so that we can be reconnected with the beautiful picture of His love, embedded within our sexuality.***

Satan's work in our lives is not just to tempt us with sin, but to infect our minds with lies that keep us from knowing God's picture of covenant love. We have absorbed millions of messages, overt and covert, reinforcing the belief that sex is all about *our* pleasure and self-expression. How can you surrender something if you don't even know it is wrong?

Unfortunately, far too often we are content with salvation while staying stuck in the world's way of thinking. God wants to not just fix our behaviors but transform our thinking so that we can be reconnected with the beautiful picture of His love, embedded within our sexuality. If you are feeling convicted or overwhelmed, don't be discouraged. It will take time to renew your mind—to recognize the lies you have believed and to replace them with the truth about God's good gift of sexuality.

This process is critically linked to—you guessed it—knowing Jesus. "I am the way, the truth, and the life." Jesus did not just claim to speak truth, but to embody truth. As you build an intimate friendship with Christ, He will expose the lies you believe and replace them with His beautiful truth.

*Lord Jesus, we are desperate for You, trapped in thinking that limits our surrender and understanding of Your goodness. Please draw us into intimacy with You that we may know You and the truth that sets us free.*

### Application Exercise:

Look at this chart. In each row, circle the statement that best describes how you think about the purpose of sexuality, marriage, and gender:

| We Are Creators: | We Are Creatures: |
|---|---|
| You must follow your romantic and sexual desires to find happiness. | What we choose is more important than what we feel. Sexual attractions and desires may come and go, but they don't define us or bring us long-term happiness. |
| Love is primarily a feeling that you cannot change. It's not an action or choice. | Covenant love is a decision, not a feeling. Within covenant, you work on sexual chemistry, feelings of love, and friendship. |

| | |
|---|---|
| You should get married only if you are sexually attracted to and fall in love with someone. | Getting married is a choice to honor God by living out the picture of the marriage covenant and family. Falling in love and sexual attraction are not wrong, but are not the foundation of a godly marriage. |
| Sexual activity is mostly for personal satisfaction and self-expression. If sex happens to involve marriage or having children by your personal choice, great, but the purpose of sex has little or nothing to do with marriage and procreation. | Sexual activity is a unique way to remember and celebrate covenant and to create new life. |
| Gender is a social construct or internal understanding of self that may or may not line up with your biological sex. | Male and female are the only two categories of biological sex and gender. They were created to uniquely reflect God's nature and are not interchangeable in personhood or the covenant of marriage. |

Looking over your answers, how has wrong thinking about the purpose of sex created confusion for you in navigating real-life issues of sexuality and gender?

A major theme of this chapter is that God reveals Himself through His creation. Reflect on your current experiences and circumstances around sexuality. Which best represents you?

- ☐ I am single and content
- ☐ I am single and experiencing deep longings
- ☐ I am in a significant dating relationship
- ☐ I am married and thriving

- ☐ I am married and struggling
- ☐ I have been through a divorce or betrayal

How does your current experience of sexuality (the good and the bad) reveal elements of God's covenant love?

## Passages to Study:

---

***Read Romans 1:18–32.***

What does Paul write about people rejecting the Creator and worshiping created things?

How did having the wrong relationship with the Creator lead to wrong *thinking* (see vv. 21–22, 25)?

How does the cultural lie that "you are the creator" impact your thinking about sexuality and sexual morality?

***Read Ephesians 2:1–3, Ephesians 4:17–19, Colossians 2:8, and Romans 12:2.***

What do these verses say about the importance of how we think about sexuality?

In what ways are you working to transform your thinking as an act of surrender to God?

## Questions for personal reflection and discussion:

1. Why do you think it is important to talk about the purpose of our sexuality?
2. In what ways have you tried to address wrong sexual behavior while still clinging to a worldly understanding of the purpose of sex?
3. React to this statement: While culture paints sexuality as a journey of self-discovery and expression, the Bible presents it as a journey of God-discovery and revelation.
4. What do you think this means: "God created sexuality to reveal the nature of His covenant love"? How is this purpose different from what you might have heard before about God's purpose for sexuality?
5. How does this purpose change your understanding of how to honor God with your sexuality?
6. In what ways do you recognize the spiritual warfare around your own sexuality?
7. What does it practically look like to surrender your thinking about sexuality and gender to the authority and love of Jesus?

CHAPTER 4

# Surrendered Sin

Now we come to the chapter you were expecting when you picked up this book. How does knowing Christ change a person's sexual behavior? Does God really care if you live with your boyfriend, look at porn, experiment with a same-sex relationship, or flirt with your married coworker?

Being a Christian means that we are called to make different sexual choices than the rest of the world. You cannot be a faithful follower of Christ without bringing your sexual thoughts and behaviors under His lordship. Our sexual choices are important to God and represent a primary way that we are set apart from the world.

As you read the Bible, you will see the writers addressing sexual issues in almost every book in the New Testament. While this is a consistent theme in the Bible, it's one that can be hard for us to embrace. We sometimes cringe at the topic of Christian sexuality because it can feel like God is condemning us for failing to live pure lives. Maybe you fear that God's standard for you is impossible to achieve, so you'd rather just not think about it.

## SEXUAL INTEGRITY

When we talk about biblical sexuality, we've often used the term "sexual purity" as the goal. That sounds like we need to be perfect. Sexual purity can feel like a pass-fail test. As you've been reading through this book, you may even have a sinking feeling about the entire conversation of surrendered sexuality because you've already concluded that you are failing. But what's the alternative? Does God grade on a curve, giving us grace and leniency when we sin?

I'm not sure "sexual purity" is the most helpful term as you think about surrendering your sexuality. Here's why. The Bible says that our purity has nothing to do with our sexual behavior, but that we become pure (morally perfect) through trusting the gift of righteousness purchased for us by Jesus' death on the cross. Your purity is about what the Bible calls "justification," which has been settled by the blood of Christ. You are justified when you put your trust in Christ Jesus regardless of your sexual behavior. This means that the person who "saves sex for marriage" but doesn't have a relationship with God through Christ is *impure*, while the person who has a rap sheet of sexual sin but gives his or her life to Christ becomes pure (justified). The Bible also talks about "sanctification," which is the process of getting free from sin and becoming holy.

I've found it more helpful to think about the goal of Christian sexuality as a journey of "sexual integrity." The word "integrity" implies wholeness—you don't have pockets of your life that are inconsistent with your relationship with God. God's call on your life is to continually integrate His truth into every area of your life, including your sexuality. Your journey of pleasing God is not about avoiding a particular act (e.g., sex outside of marriage), but is an ongoing commitment to honor Him with everything. Sexual integrity is a journey of surrender. None of us naturally do this perfectly, but as we learn to surrender, our sexuality becomes more and more aligned with God's purposes.

There is a reason this chapter is preceded by three chapters and followed by four more. What you've already read gives you the reason *why* our sexual integrity is so important. Because of who God is and because of how He has redeemed us, we live a different kind of life. Just as importantly, what you will read in future chapters will point you to the encouragement you need in order to walk toward sexual wholeness.

We should never preach a Christian sexual ethic apart from the greater message of the gospel. We were lost and hopeless in our sin. Christ died to reconcile us to Himself, forgiving all of our sin, even our sexual sin. We are now on the journey of learning to live surrendered lives, for His glory and by the power of His grace and mercy toward us.

## WHY CHRISTIANS HAVE A DIFFERENT SEXUAL ETHIC

People will often ask me questions like, "What's wrong with two consenting adults having sex? They aren't hurting anyone."

Our culture understands sexual morality based on ownership and consent. Because you own your body, you are the only one who can give consent. You have the right to use your body for *your purposes.*

> ***God is not just a helpful advisor in our sex lives. He is co-owner, as His Spirit lives inside us.***

As Christians, we also understand the principle of ownership and the importance of consent, but we recognize that God owns your body too. When you trusted Christ for your salvation, you gave Him your body. You've probably heard that "your body is the temple of the Holy Spirit," but you most likely have applied this to the importance of taking care of your physical health.

In Paul's letter to the Corinthians, he reminded them that Christ purchased not only their salvation, but also their bodies.

He explains this in 1 Corinthians 6:13–20 (NLT):

> You say, "Food was made for the stomach, and the stomach for food." (This is true, though someday God will do away with both of them.) But you can't say that our bodies were made for sexual immorality. They were made for the Lord, and the Lord cares about our bodies. And God will raise us from the dead by his power, just as he raised our Lord from the dead.
>
> Don't you realize that your bodies are actually parts of Christ? Should a man take his body, which is part of Christ, and join it to a prostitute? Never! And don't you realize that if a man joins himself to a prostitute, he becomes one body with her? For the Scriptures say, "The two are united into one." But the person who is joined to the Lord is one spirit with him.
>
> Run from sexual sin! No other sin so clearly affects the body as this one does. For sexual immorality is a sin against your own body. Don't you realize that your body is the temple of the Holy Spirit, who lives in you and was given to you by God? You do not belong to yourself, for God bought you with a high price. So you must honor God with your body.

Paul clarifies that he is not primarily talking about our physical health because what we eat and our physical flesh will die and be resurrected one day. But God really cares about how we use our bodies sexually. We have a covenant with God, and that covenant means that we belong to Him. God is not just a helpful advisor in our sex lives. He is co-owner, as His Spirit lives inside us. That means we don't do whatever we want with our sexuality but that we surrender our bodies for *His purposes.*

This would be like cosigning a house with a friend. Legally, you both would have to agree to sell the house to someone else. God does not violate your will by making you do things with your body. In the same way, you are not to violate His will by making sexual choices that ignore or dishonor

Him. Our desire to honor God with our sexuality should be even greater as we realize His goodness and holiness. He can see past our feelings and current circumstances and is eternally wise in His will for us.

Again, "You do not belong to yourself, for God bought you with a high price. So you must honor God with your body" (1 Cor. 6:19–20 NLT).

We glorify God with our bodies by stewarding our sexuality consistently with His design. The first step to honoring God with our sexuality is to recognize and "run from" (v. 18) sexual sin. In this chapter, we are going to address what sexual sin is and how to surrender it.

What you are about to read is going to be in direct contradiction to the cultural messages that surround you. Remember that to be a disciple of Jesus means that we live for God's glory, trusting Him with our lives. Don't read this chapter as a pass-fail test, but as an encouragement to understand God's will for your life and to surrender to His love and power as you seek to please Him.

## WHAT IS SEXUAL SIN?

To put it simply, all sexual sin is the "misuse" of the gift of sex—using sex for our own purposes rather than surrendering to God's purpose. Here are four specific ways that we can sin sexually:

### *1. Separating sex from covenant*

The most common way we sin sexually is to separate sex from covenant. God created sex to be like a three-strand braided rope, intertwining the physical expression of sexual intimacy with the relational commitment of covenant and the spiritual backdrop of God's blessing. The most beautiful picture of this is in the Song of Songs where the bride and groom celebrate their covenant with great passion and sexual love, and God speaks over them, "Eat, friends, and drink; drink your fill of love" (5:1). You see all three strands of physical passion, relational covenant, and God's blessing!

God made sex to be a powerful, sensual, bonding expression of the full giving of husband and wife as a reflection of His love for us. Sexual sin unwinds these three strands of the rope, separating the physical act of sex from the covenant of marriage. When you engage in sexual sin, you are also separating yourself from the presence and purpose of God in your sexuality.

We separate sex from covenant in premarital sex of any kind and extramarital affairs.

### 2. *Using people for sex*

The second way we sin sexually is objectifying and using people for our own pleasure. We approach someone based on our appetites rather than honoring them. The most straightforward example of this is prostitution. You pay to borrow someone's body for your personal gratification, without any regard for the well-being of the person you are defiling.

Jesus said that our lustful thoughts toward someone are just as sinful as sexual acts. This means that we sinfully use people when we look at pornography, sext someone, or linger in sexual thoughts about anyone (other than our spouse). Unfortunately, many of us have normalized sexually objectifying people in our conversation, like so-called locker-room talk or girl talk that reduces someone to their sexual status or attractiveness.

You can also sinfully objectify your spouse within marriage. You can misuse the gift of sex within your covenant relationship. For example, let's say you struggle with pornography. Though physically, you are having sex with your spouse, your thoughts and attitudes are directed toward your own sinful appetites. You're not making love as an expression of your covenant, but using your spouse as an outlet. Not all married sex is honoring God.

### 3. *Disregarding the importance of gender in sex*

We sin sexually when we honor the principle of covenant, but we ignore the importance of gender in God's gift of sexuality. Remember that Jesus defined the purpose for marriage and sex, referring back to creation with gender-specific terms: "For this reason a man will leave his father and mother and be united to his wife, and the two will become one flesh" (Matt. 19:5).

We ignore the importance of the Creator's design when we treat gender as interchangeable either in our identity or within our sexual relationships. This would include same-sex marriage, as well as rejecting our biological sex in pursuit of our own expression of gender. As you likely know, the topics of same-sex marriage and gender fluidity are very controversial and deeply painful for those walking through same-sex attraction or gender dysphoria. Experiencing confusion with sexual attraction or gender is not a sin. James makes this clear when he describes the interplay between temptation, desires, and sin. "Each person is tempted when they are dragged away by their own evil desires and enticed. Then, after desire has conceived, it gives birth to sin; and sin, when it is full-grown, gives birth to death" (James 1:14–15).

We all have evil desires based on our sinful nature. While we don't get to decide what temptations and wounds we battle, we are responsible for how we respond to those struggles. The spiritual battle requires us to surrender our evil desires, whatever they may be, rather than nurturing them.

#### *4. Failing to honor the covenant of marriage*

God did not design you for "serial monogamy." It's not okay to keep sex within covenant, but to hop from covenant to covenant until you find one that satisfies you. Jesus said, "Moses permitted you to divorce your wives because your hearts were hard. But it was not this way from the beginning. I tell you that anyone who divorces his wife, except for sexual immorality, and marries another woman commits adultery" (Matt. 19:8–9). Divorce itself is not always a sin. There are times when a covenant has been so violated that divorce is the only viable option. This is why God includes provisions in the Bible for people in these circumstances.

As you learned in the last chapter, the covenant of marriage is the earthly picture of God's enduring love for us. This means that married Christians are to take very seriously their vows "until death do us part" and to treat each other with the love of Christ—with kindness, forgiveness, and compassion. The topic of divorce and remarriage is controversial within Christian circles, but we need to talk about it as it directly relates to how we honor God with our sexuality.

✦ ✦ ✦

Each one of these categories of sin represents deep pain and struggle. It's easy to say, "That's a sin!" when it's not your particular battle. We can also be tempted to minimize God's holiness related to our own sexual sin, past or present. Knowing Jesus should humble each of us in our sin, give us compassion for others, and encourage us to live in the freedom He purchased for us.

## HOW TO RESPOND TO OUR SIN

Just recently I was walking with a dear friend who had confessed to me significant sexual sin. She was in the deep end of the grief and consequences of her sin and said to me, "I have nothing to bring to Jesus. I am totally dependent upon His mercy."

In the following days, as I reflected on this conversation, the Holy Spirit showed me my own sin—more hidden and "respectable," but just as great of an offense to our holy God. As Billy Graham famously said, "The ground is level at the foot of the cross."[1] To be a Christian means that we live daily with a deep awareness of our need for God's saving grace.

There is not a person on earth who has not violated God's design and purpose for sex. And if you are thinking, "But my sin isn't as bad as my divorced brother or my trans sister," remember the story Jesus told about the religious leader and the tax collector in Luke 18, how He treated those who accused the woman of adultery in John 8, and His rebuke of Simon the

Pharisee when he judged the woman who had "lived a sinful life" in Luke 7. Our spiritual pride is more damaging to our souls than even our sexual sin because it blinds us to our need for God.

When the Holy Spirit convicts us of sin (sexual or otherwise), we have a very clear path to health and wholeness.

### *Recognize your sin*

As obvious as it may sound, we can't deal with sin until we call it what it is. In 1973, Christian psychiatrist Karl Menninger wrote a book called *Whatever Became of Sin?* His thesis is that our society and mental health are suffering because we refuse to be honest about our sin. He writes, "If we speak of our own sins, we are usually being humorously self-indulgent or pretentiously pious; few of us are very shamefaced in any such confession."[2]

Instead of facing our sin, we . . .

**Minimize it.** "Sending nudes on a text is not that big of a deal. It's not like we slept together."

**Excuse it.** "I've waited for God to bring me a spouse, but He isn't hearing my prayers." "He made me this way."

**Blame others.** "I didn't grow up with good role models." "What is a guy supposed to do when women walk around wearing practically nothing?"

**Compare our sin with others.** "Everyone I know sleeps together in a dating relationship, but we waited six months until we knew we loved each other."

Sin is spiritually dangerous, but we act as if the poison can't get to us if we don't name it. That would be like taking fentanyl and going to the emergency room because of life-threatening side effects but refusing to tell anyone what is causing them. Eventually, the truth will come out, but your denial may mean you waited far too long to get help.

***Confess your sin***

When you recognize your sin, but you don't confess it, you are likely to be tortured with shame and guilt. John tells us that unconfessed sin gets in the way of your relationship with God and with other people (1 John 1:6; Ps. 32:1–5). You were not meant to carry the weight of unconfessed sin.

Confessing your sin begins with being honest with God. Instead of beating around the bush, it means telling Him what He already knows. Pour out your heart to Him. I once read a convicting challenge from A. W. Tozer for me to call my sin by its worst name.[3] Instead of minimizing and rationalizing with God, I want to give the fullest confession that I can, so that I might receive the deepest outpouring of His compassion, mercy, and grace.

But our confession, to be complete, doesn't end with God.

*Perhaps we have so little freedom and healing among Christians because we have so little true confession.*

James reminds us of the importance of confessing our sins to each other. "Confess your sins to each other and pray for each other so that you may be healed" (James 5:16). Perhaps we have so little freedom and healing among Christians because we have so little true confession.

Not every Christian is a safe place for you to confess your sin—particularly sexual sin. But there are times when God provides us a safe place to confess, and we don't have the courage to step into it.

Maybe you've been seeing a counselor for months, talking about your anxiety and your loneliness but keeping your porn use a secret. Or you are half-heartedly trying to work on your marriage while nurturing a "harmless" flirtation with a friend. Or you've been dancing around discussions in your accountability group about struggles but being too vague to be vulnerable.

While God forgives your sin when you confess it to Him, healing involves being vulnerable with the safe people He brings into your life. We need to walk with other Christians who can pray for us, encourage us, and remind us of God's grace as we battle sin.

**While God forgives your sin when you confess it to Him, healing involves being vulnerable with the safe people He brings into your life.**

***Believe in God's grace and forgiveness***

"Several years ago, I had an affair that led to a pregnancy," Amanda said. "I was so afraid that my husband would know the baby wasn't his that I had an abortion. My secret sin felt like an invisible wall between me and God. Last year, I finally confessed my sin to my husband. We are in the process of healing. In my head, I know that God forgives me, but will I always live with this deep, deep shame?"

Like my friend Amanda, your past sin might feel like a massive weight. You've recognized and confessed your sin, but you still carry the shame of it. But Galatians 5:1 states, "It is for freedom that Christ has set us free."

Either Christ died to carry your sin and shame or He didn't. There is no halfway. As much as you may feel like you have to punish yourself for your sin, this is not God's will for you. Christ died for your freedom—not only from sin, but from the shame of your sin. His will is freedom!

Sometimes the relational, emotional, and physical consequences of our sin can haunt us. In Amanda's situation, it took time for her husband to forgive and for their marriage to heal. Sexual sin can leave in its wake deep sorrow, broken relationships, and STDs. But let those shadows remind you of the greater consquences God has saved you from.

King David committed an infamous sexual sin with Bathsheba, another man's wife. He had a lifetime of consequences, yet understood God's eternal redemption from his sin. You can read about it in 2 Samuel 11. David repented and later gratefully wrote,

> The LORD is compassionate and gracious,
> slow to anger, abounding in love.
> He will not always accuse,
> nor will he harbor his anger forever;
> he does not treat us as our sins deserve
> or repay us according to our iniquities.
> For as high as the heavens are above the earth,
> so great is his love for those who fear him;
> as far as the east is from the west,
> so far has he removed our transgressions from us. (Ps. 103:8–12)

Your integrity as a follower of Christ involves not only how you behave sexually, but also how fully you believe that God has forgiven you. If you are walking in a cloud of shame, you have not fully surrendered yourself to God. You may have convinced yourself that feeling guilty for the rest of your life is your way of telling God how sorry you are. If you want to honor God in the wake of your sin, believe Him when He declares that you are forgiven, and then spend the rest of your life telling people about His great mercy and love toward you.

***Turn from your sin***

One day, some religious leaders literally caught a woman committing adultery and dragged her (probably half-naked) before Jesus. Jesus forgave the woman, silenced her accusers, and then said this, "Leave your life of sin" (John 8:11).

God's grace doesn't mean we can just go on sinning because Jesus paid for our sins. I remember talking to one woman who was thinking about having sex with her boyfriend. She said, "Yes, I know it's wrong. But I also know God will understand and forgive me." This is a dangerous way for us to think and shows how little we understand what God's grace actually is. *Grace does not mean we take sin lightly but that we take God seriously.* Yes, getting free from sin can be a long battle, and God is gracious even when we fail. However, God's grace should never be used for an excuse to give in to sin and temptation. The Hebrew and Greek words the Bible uses for repentance mean "to turn" or "to have another mind."[4] Repentance is not just being sorry, but changing our direction because of Christ's love.

## HOW WE GET STUCK IN SIN

Maybe you've tried to turn from your sexual sin only to find yourself back in the same behavior you've confessed a hundred times. All sin, including sexual sin, can be more deeply rooted in us than we realize. Maybe as you are reading this book, you feel like God is shining a spotlight on that sin pattern you know you need to surrender, but you can't figure out how. I find it encouraging that even the apostle Paul felt this way sometimes. He wrote, "What I want to do, I don't do. I end up doing what I hate!" (Rom. 7:15, paraphrased).

Have you ever felt this way? Sometimes we get stuck in sin because we try to stop the sinful behavior without dealing with underlying attitudes and strongholds that keep us tied to the sin. I remember a season in my life where I was trying not to gossip. I heard a sermon about the power of my words to bring life or death, and I really wanted to stop saying things that hurt other people. The Lord began to show me that I could discipline my tongue, but my heart was the true problem. I say things because I think them and I think them because my heart is proud. I might have the self-control to restrain my words most of the time, but if my heart is judgmental and critical, those thoughts will eventually come out of me. "For the mouth speaks what the heart is full of" (Luke 6:45).

I needed Jesus to give me a new heart, not just a muzzle for my mouth.

The same thing is true in our struggle with sexual sin. We sin with our bodies because our hearts are sinful. Sin is not just what we *do,* it is also what we *want.* This is why Jesus' work in our lives has to go way deeper than just our actions. It's not going to be effective to deal with your sexual sin only as it involves your behavior.

***Most Christians try to cut off temptation at the point of action rather than learning to surrender their desires to the Lord.***

God created sexual desire as a very good thing. The world would be a very sterile (and eventually empty) place without sexual desire. But like every other good gift, our experience of sexual desire has been tainted by sin and the brokenness of our world. Every one of us has desires that should not just be channeled into marriage, but rather to be surrendered to the purposes and righteousness of God.

Our desires can be "deceitful," meaning they don't always tell us the truth. In the moment of temptation, what feels life-giving can actually be what will bring death. Why do you *want* to look at porn? Why do you *want* to entice that guy to desire you sexually? Why do you *want* to move in together instead of getting married? Why do you *want* to demand sex from your spouse? These may be normal human desires, but normal doesn't mean they are right desires.

Most Christians try to cut off temptation at the point of action rather than learning to surrender their desires to the Lord. This is why it is so important not just to understand that our sexual actions can be sinful, but also that our thoughts and desires can be wrong. If you walk around believing that you must have some sexual or romantic experience to be fulfilled, that belief is just as sinful as the actions it might lead to. We honor God with our sexuality by confessing and surrendering the desire that leads to sin, asking the Lord to replace that desire with His perspective.

Very often, the roots of our sin are tied to strongholds of loss, fear, wounds, and trauma. Satan takes the hard things in our lives and plants seeds that mess with our longings and desires. If you can relate to that, we will dive into what it looks like to surrender our wounds in the next chapter.

God wants to do a deeper work in your heart than freeing you from sinful sexual behavior. Remember, you are a new creation in Christ Jesus. While the "old self" still hangs around with its deceitful desires, God created you to live with new desires, with a "new self" rooted in His love and the power of the Holy Spirit. Learning how to do this is a process of . . . you guessed it—surrendering.

## HOW DO YOU FLEE FROM SEXUAL SIN?

In 1 Thessalonians 4:3–5, Paul tells the early Christians, "It is God's will that you should be sanctified: that you should avoid sexual immorality; that each of you should learn to control your own body in a way that is holy and honorable, not in passionate lust like the pagans, who do not know God." Paul uses the word "sanctification," which is the ongoing process of being purified and freed from sin. Honoring God with your sexuality involves the continual choice to live by the will and Spirit of God (the new self) rather than being driven by your flesh (the old self).

I love that Paul presents this as a process of maturity, "learning" to control your body and passions. Once you become a Christian, you don't automatically know how to respond to sexual temptations, particularly with sin that has been a part of your life for a long time. This means that you need to be discipled in your sexuality.

Overcoming sexual sin in your life is not a single action but learning to reorder your thinking and your environment. You can lose your battle with sin before the temptation even hits. For example, a Christian couple dating might spend hours alone together late at night making out and then trying to hold the line of not having sex. This couple has set themselves up for failure. While they may not have crossed the line of intercourse, they are treating each other without the wisdom and respect to proactively address temptation.

The same is true of someone who battles with porn. He or she promises never to look at it again, but is surrounded by unfiltered devices, is relationally isolated, and has never been truly honest with anyone about the extent of the struggle. This person has already lost the battle with sin.

Just as you can stay stuck in sin when you don't proactively surrender, you can also overcome the battle with sin before you even face the temptation. Here's how:

***Ruthlessly get rid of what makes you stumble***

Jesus said, "If your right eye causes you to stumble, gouge it out and throw it away. It is better for you to lose one part of your body than for your whole body to be thrown into hell. And if your right hand causes you to stumble, cut it off and throw it away. It is better for you to lose one part of your body than for your whole body to go into hell" (Matt. 5:29–30).

Scholars agree that Jesus was using hyperbole to make a point: He wasn't calling us to literally poke out our eyes or cut off our hands, yet the seriousness of His statement often gets discounted. Jesus' teaching that we cut off our right hand is a figure of speech that means that you may need to get rid of things (and relationships) that actually have "life" in them. Sometimes we need to surrender good things that have become an entryway of sinful temptations. In *The Cost of Discipleship*, Dietrich Bonhoeffer writes, "No sacrifice is too great if it enables us to conquer a lust which cuts us off from Jesus."[5]

The problem is that most of us *flirt* with sin instead of *fleeing* from it.

We don't want the pain and inconvenience of cutting off the source of our temptation, and so we lie to ourselves. "I am strong enough to handle it. I'll know when to draw the line." There will always be excuses and reasons why we hang on to things we need to get rid of.

Getting serious about surrendering your sexuality means courageously cutting off the relationships, comforts, and patterns in your life that set you up for sin. In order to get rid of porn, you might need to switch to a "dumb phone." If you want to honor your marriage vows, that might mean changing churches to get away from a relational temptation. Likewise, you will not be able to obey God with your sexual thoughts while bingeing shows and music that continually display the exact opposite.

***Surround yourself with people and practices that remind you of your identity in Christ***

"Those who live according to the flesh have their minds set on what the flesh desires; but those who live in accordance with the Spirit have their minds set on what the Spirit desires" (Rom. 8:5).

What you think about matters, and what you are surrounded by determines what you think about. Our thought patterns are shaped and informed by the people, influences, and messages that surround us. This can have either a positive or negative impact on your journey of surrender.

Just as we cut off things and relationships that keep us stuck in sin, we can also choose to include people and practices that help us keep our thoughts on Christ. You may make choices like listening to worship music (Eph. 5:19), getting together with other Christians, and pursuing a godly mentor.

Spiritual disciplines like fasting can also be an effective way to learn to control your body. Our appetites demand our attention. Even while writing this paragraph, my stomach is telling me it's time to eat, distracting me from what I'm trying to do. We can tell our bodies no when our wills are set on something more important. We live in such an immediate gratification culture that we need to practice saying no to what our flesh is screaming for.

Like a growling stomach, your experience of intense sexual desire will pass if you wait it out. You can exercise that "muscle" of recognizing desire and denying yourself by starting with food. When you skip a meal or fast from sugar for a month, you are learning to say no to your immediate physical desires.

Spiritual fasting is not just what we say no to, but also what we say yes to. We fast so we can feast. The goal isn't just to deny ourselves sex, but to become more alive to the greater joy of knowing God.

Our greatest victory over temptation comes when we want God more than we desire our sin. Your sexual temptations are so powerful because they have come to represent something you deeply desire. Sin is always an illegitimate way to meet legitimate desires. You want peace. Love. To be noticed. An escape from pain. Pleasure. To be known and safe in a relationship. There is a kernel of something good and important in every one of our desires. **God is not in competition with these desires but is the completion of them.**

*Our problem is that we have come to see the source of our sin as more trustworthy than God.*

Our problem is that we have come to see the source of our sin as more trustworthy than God. Surrendering your sexuality doesn't mean denying your desires, but that you bring them to the Lord, trusting that He will satisfy them. If we turn from our sin without turning to our Savior, we will live in despair.

But if we go to God with our desires, we will find more than we could ever imagine. Scripture is filled with the testimony of people who have experienced this. David praised the Lord throughout the Psalms, declaring that God satisfies our desires with *good things* (Ps. 103:5)! Paul was so confident in this truth that he wrote, "This same God who takes care of me will supply all your needs from his glorious riches, which have been given to us in Christ Jesus" (Phil. 4:19 NLT).

As you finish this chapter, the goodness of God may feel like a far-off comfort compared to your struggle with sin. My friend, don't give up, and don't get discouraged. God not only sees you in your battle with sin, He is your Helper through it.

I remember feeling very discouraged in my own battle with sin, frustrated that I seemed to fall into it again and again. Then I read these verses from Jude:

> Now to him who is able to keep you from stumbling and to present you blameless before the presence of his glory with great joy, to the only God, our Savior, through Jesus Christ our Lord, be glory, majesty, dominion, and authority, before all time and now and forever. (Jude 24–25 ESV[6])

***Don't keep your eyes fixed on your battle with sin. Keep your eyes fixed on the One who loves you, who advocates for you, and who is your freedom and righteousness.***

All of a sudden I realized that Jesus is able to keep me from sin. He is able to free me from my flesh. And He is able to present me to God the Father without sin and without fault! I can't do this myself, but I believe that Jesus is working His righteousness in me as I surrender more and more to His presence in my life. Years ago, this verse was just an encouraging thought, but now, I am experiencing it as a reality. The persistent choice to surrender and to trust in Jesus is changing me! C. S. Lewis wrote,

> We may, indeed, be sure that perfect chastity—like perfect charity—will not be attained by any merely human efforts. You must ask for God's help. Even when you have done so, it may seem to you for a long

> time that no help, or less help than you need, is being given. Never mind. After each failure, ask forgiveness, pick yourself up, and try again. Very often what God first helps us towards is not the virtue itself but just this power of always trying again. For however important chastity (or courage, or truthfulness, or any other virtue) may be, this process trains us in habits of the soul which are more important still. It cures our illusions about ourselves and teaches us to depend on God.[7]

My dear friend, the goal is not to have less sin, but to have more of Jesus. Don't keep your eyes fixed on your battle with sin. Keep your eyes fixed on the One who loves you, who advocates for you, and who is your freedom and righteousness.

### Application Exercise:

---

What is the specific sexual sin you struggle with?

How is that sexual sin an "illegitimate way to address legitimate needs"?

Check the ways that sin or relationship "serves" you:

- ☐ Helps me deal with my loneliness
- ☐ Is a way to temporarily reduce negative emotions like anger, anxiety, or sadness
- ☐ Makes me feel valued or loved

In what ways have you tried to stop the sin without addressing the underlying needs it represents? What would it practically look like for you to bring those needs to the Lord in the process of surrendering your sin?

## Passages to Study:

---

***Read Ephesians 2:1–2, Ephesians 4:22–24, Romans 1:21–25, and 1 Peter 2:11.***

What do each of these passages say about how sin has impacted our desires and thoughts?

Why is it important to surrender our sinful thoughts and desires about sexuality?

Do you agree that our battle with sin involves not just what we *do* but also things we may *desire*? Why or why not?

What sexual thoughts and desires is God asking you to surrender?

What happens when we deny our sinful desires without turning to God to satisfy them?

## Questions for personal reflection and discussion:

1. How is the pursuit of "sexual purity" different from "sexual integrity"?
2. How does the principle of ownership and consent impact how you think about what is right and wrong sexually?
3. How have you been using sexuality for *your purposes* instead of for God's purposes?
4. Share some examples of how you minimize, excuse, blame, or compare sexual sin instead of confessing it.
5. Why does holding on to sexual shame mean that you lack sexual integrity as a Christian?
6. How do you specifically need to "reorder your environment" to proactively address sexual sin and temptation?
7. Why is fasting an effective way to "learn to control your own body"? How has fasting from food (or something else) helped you in your journey of sexual integrity?

CHAPTER 5

# Surrendered Brokenness

One of my favorite clothing brands is Life Is Good. If I don't have to dress up for something, there is a very good chance I'm wearing a Life Is Good shirt of some kind. The slogans are lighthearted, the cotton comfortable, and the brand name positive. Yes, life is good. But it can also be very, very bad.

I began my professional counseling career while in my twenties. In a short period of time, I met with a teen who had seen his uncle shot and his mother imprisoned for prostitution, a parent whose eight-year-old son was killed by a wild animal, and a woman who had been repeatedly abused by her father.

We cannot talk about the beauty of creation or the goodness of our Creator without the profound awareness of how broken our experiences can be. As you have been reading about God's creation of sex, of gender, of intimacy, and as you have read of His desire for your freedom, I wonder if something within you rises up with an emotional and powerful objection.

## BROKENNESS: THE GAP BETWEEN YOU AND WHOLENESS

Brokenness is the barrier that keeps you from the maturity, freedom, and love you've been reading about. As you have been expanding your understanding of sexual wholeness, you likely have become even more aware of your brokenness.

You want to trust God with your sexuality, but you can't.

You want to stop looking at porn, but you don't.

You want to embrace your sexuality as a beautiful gift from God, but you have too many experiences that prove otherwise.

If teaching about biblical sexuality were as simple as helping people grasp the beauty of God's creation, all you would need to do is read a book explaining the goodness of male and female, our sexual drives and desires, and the gifts of both marriage and singleness. But it's not that simple. Unfortunately, reality gets in the way.

In our fallen world, our own bodies can seem to betray us. Even before we take our first breath, our bodies have been affected by the brokenness of this world. After speaking at a church in Denver, Jim approached and shared with me about the loneliness he experiences because of his intersex condition. (Intersex is the condition of someone born with reproductive or sexual anatomy that is not considered typical for male or female.) "When you spoke about how we are all impacted by the fall, you mentioned intersex people. My type is one of the rarest forms. Ninety percent of my doctors didn't know we existed but soon became believers when they saw my condition. Most intersex people are forced into the shadows, alone with no one they can turn to for acceptance and Christian fellowship."

Then there is the reality of evil committed against us. Perhaps no area of our humanity has been more commonly violated than human sexuality. The latest research shows that over half of women and nearly one-third of men have experienced sexual violence.[1] Those astounding numbers represent millions of untold stories of lifelong pain.

Even if you haven't experienced sexual trauma, you likely have been impacted by the objectification of your body, the shock of betrayal, unhealthy family dynamics, or the pain of rejection. Much of our brokenness comes from relationships that are meant to be safe and healing, making us leery of ever trusting again. An authority figure who abuses his position. A teacher who piles on shame or false promises. Or a spouse who keeps a devastating secret for decades.

In addition to the tidal wave of sexual harm, we also have to deal with the consequences and weight of our own sexual sin. We have been the betrayer, the one who reduced someone to a sexual object, who acted selfishly to gratify our own desires, or judged someone hypocritically.

All this brokenness makes us feel like we are on the outside looking into God's unattainable promises. *Life may be good for some people,* you think. *But not for me.*

***All this brokenness makes us feel like we are on the outside looking into God's unattainable promises.* Life may be good for some people, *you think.* But not for me.**

## WHY WE NEED TO SURRENDER SEXUAL BROKENNESS

I was recently talking with a woman who is battling disconnection in her marriage and confusion about her sexual desire. I asked her, "Have you experienced sexual trauma in your past?" She answered as I expected. "Yes. Something happened to me when I was a child, and I also was raped as a college freshman."

"Have you spent any time working through those traumas?" The answer, again as I expected, was no.

I've rarely met someone who battles extensive sexual confusion, pain, or unwanted sexual desire who doesn't have a history of sexual trauma. And far too often, their experiences of sexual pain have been buried with a "the-past-is-the-past" mentality. We seriously underestimate the impact our wounds have on our behaviors and struggles.

Sexual trauma leaves a profound mark on a person's soul, relationships, and even on their brain wiring. Tim Hein, a victim of sexual abuse, wrote an insightful book called *Understanding Sexual Abuse*. He explains that experiences of abuse, particularly within childhood and adolescence, profoundly impact how our brains develop.

> Research now indicates that survivors of abuse are statistically more likely to experience depression, anxiety-related disorders, or panic attacks, to develop eating disorders or substance dependence, to show antisocial or aggressive behavior, and to consider or attempt suicide. . . . Many survivors have difficulty concentrating, are constantly on edge, and have difficulty cultivating intimate relationships. Some throw themselves into multiple, almost arbitrary, sexual experiences, while others avoid sex altogether.[2]

Sexual trauma is also correlated with transgenderism, same-sex orientation, promiscuity, and sexual addiction.[3] I spoke with a man who runs a sexual addiction program. He told me he had never met someone with a sexual addiction who did not also have significant sexual or psychological trauma in their past.

So in addition to the shame of what happened to them, many survivors of sexual trauma have the compounding shame of trying to manage feelings and behaviors that feel very much out of their control.

Brian was groomed and sexually abused by his high school baseball coach. Because of the shame and confusion he felt, Brian never shared with anyone about what happened to him.

> I felt gross about what happened to me, and I dreamed about it often. I was so confused about my sexual identity. Was I gay? Bisexual? I thought I must be if I let a man do that to me and enjoyed it. So, I became very

> promiscuous in high school and through my young adult years. I used women sexually to bolster my sexual identity. I used them the way my coach had used me. I already felt so dirty and guilty that I told myself it didn't matter anymore if I piled on more guilt. I never told any of this to anyone before telling my wife. She could tell I was distant and cold when we were intimate. Our sex life was in shambles.[4]

One woman I interviewed for this book shared candidly how difficult it is to surrender her sexual sin to the Lord because of the tangled thoughts and experiences of past brokenness:

> From the time I was thirteen, my boyfriend began sexual interactions that, like it or not, conditioned my body to respond. This started a massive struggle between what I knew was right and wrong and my body's response to sexual experiences. It tore me in half and resulted in self-harm, eating disorders, and other harmful behaviors. Then, in my marriage, my now ex-husband used sex to manipulate and harm me.
>
> When addressing the sinful choices or sin pattern in my life, now I'm working against subconscious responses that have happened for the last thirty years. I'm learning that there are chemical and physical and subconscious influences of things that have happened to me that make sexual integrity far more difficult. Sometimes I find myself responding sexually to someone even when it's the last thing I would want to do. All of this happens while I'm trying to be a good Christian. Shame and guilt have caused me to give up completely sometimes.

Maybe you can relate.

It is cruel to tell someone to fix their sexual behavior without compassionately addressing the deep wounds from their past.

The Bible tells us that Jesus is your Healer, your Comforter, and your

Counselor. He is not just sitting up in heaven judging your behavior. He is at the door of your heart with the intention of restoring you.

## SEXUAL BROKENNESS CAN KEEP US FROM KNOWING JESUS

In a bitter twist, our sexual wounds not only set us up for unwanted desires, shame, and discouragement, but they also often keep us from the ultimate source of our healing.

Morgan shared, "I was raised in the Christian church and my understanding of sexuality was really the 'shoulds' and the many 'should nots' of engaging others sexually. I believed that if I made choices within God's rules, sexuality with my spouse would be the most intimate human/spiritual experience. Instead, it has been the source of significant challenge and hardship for us both. As a result, I don't trust God's way to bring fulfillment, and I don't want to surrender to it. At this point, my sexual questions, trauma, longings, and disappointments have drawn me away from God."

We need to understand that there is a very real spiritual battle occurring beneath our own personal journeys with sexuality. That battle may feel like it's about sex. Sex is the pain point, but what is at stake is far more important. Satan's goal is not to keep you from a wonderful marriage or sexual experience. His ultimate goal is to set up "strongholds" that keep you from an intimate relationship with Jesus.

As Morgan shared, sexual brokenness isn't just about sex. Sexual pain causes us to question the goodness and trustworthiness of God. Questions about sex will lead us to questions about God.

In 2 Corinthians 10:3–5, Paul helps the early church understand the spiritual battle beneath their circumstances. He wrote,

> For though we live in the world, we do not wage war as the world does. The weapons we fight with are not the weapons of the world. On the

> contrary, they have divine power to demolish strongholds. We demolish arguments and every pretension that sets itself up against the knowledge of God, and we take captive every thought to make it obedient to Christ.

Although we live in fleshly bodies and feel human emotions, something spiritual is happening beneath the struggles we experience. Notice how Paul says that the "strongholds" set themselves up against the knowledge of God. When Paul uses that word "knowledge," he is referring to intimately knowing, trusting, and experiencing God. The strongholds he refers to are arguments and thought patterns that keep us from that intimate relationship with God.

Even as you've read this book, you probably resonate with what one person shared. "I know in my head that this is all true, but it just doesn't feel true in my heart. I know how to say all the right things and can even point to the Bible verses that back them up. I want to trust God with my sexuality, but I'm just not there yet. I guess it comes down to that I'm just not convinced that God really wants me to be fulfilled and happy."

As you have been learning, the gift of sexual intimacy and marriage are temporary, earthly experiences that point us to a greater, eternal reality. The goal of Christian sexual wholeness is *not* to live a sin-free, blissful life, experiencing great sex. The goal of Christian sexual wholeness is that instead of sexuality being something that keeps us from God, it becomes something that reveals and draws us closer to God.

Your past sexual abuse is not the stronghold. Nor is your spouse's betrayal, your history of sexual sin, your same-sex desire, or your pastor's sexual failure. Those are events through which Satan likely embedded strongholds.

Our strongholds usually show up in the form of questions that represent our doubt in the power and goodness of God. Dane Ortlund explains,

"The fall . . . entrenched in our minds dark thoughts of God, thoughts that are only dug out over multiple exposures to the gospel over many years. Perhaps Satan's greatest victory in your life today is not the sin in which you regularly indulge but the dark thoughts of God's heart that cause you to go there in the first place and keep you cool toward him in the wake of it."[5]

As we will see, some of the people who knew and loved Jesus most intimately wrestled with strongholds in their experience of pain and brokenness.

### *Mary and Martha asked, "Where were you?"*

Although Jesus loved everyone when He was on earth, He formed a deep friendship with a group of three siblings, Mary, Martha, and Lazarus. All their friends knew Jesus had a special love for this family, which is why everyone was so confused when Lazarus became sick and Jesus did not arrive in time to heal him. What happens next is one of the most moving recorded events in Jesus' life on earth (John 11).

Mary and Martha sent a message to Jesus telling Him about Lazarus' illness, asking Him to come and heal him. Mysteriously, Jesus didn't respond, and Lazarus ended up dying. It wasn't until He got word of His friend's death that Jesus made His way to the family's home. Both Mary and Martha greeted their friend with the same gut-wrenching accusation: "If you had come, our brother would not have died." Beneath their sorrow were honest questions: "Where were you? Why didn't You come? Don't You love us?"

Maybe you wonder about your own situation. God could have shielded you from the abuse. He could have given you a fulfilling marriage or protected you from one that was destructive. Where was He?

### *Paul asked, "Why don't you?"*

The apostle Paul, the very one I've so often referenced throughout this book, had a problem. It may have been a battle with a particular temptation, a physical ailment, or a deep insecurity. We don't know what it was, but

Paul described it as a "thorn in my flesh, a messenger of Satan, to torment me" (2 Cor. 12:7). This description tells us that Paul's problem wasn't trivial, but something that interfered with his daily life and made him feel weak.

*I wonder if, in your own brokenness, you sometimes doubt the very truth you have committed your life to speaking. I know I have.*

Paul, who wrote so many encouraging letters about the victory we have in Christ Jesus, asked God to give him a victory by taking away this tormenting problem. The Lord said, "No."

As faithful as Paul was, and as intimately as he knew Jesus, why would God not rescue him from the "thorn" that tormented him?

Have you ever asked why God doesn't take away your unwanted sexual desires, your temptation, or your limitation?

### *John the Baptist asked, "Are you really the Messiah?"*

John the Baptist was set apart even before he was born to be the prophet who prepared the way for the Messiah, his cousin Jesus. John was courageous and absolutely committed to his mission. Jesus said that he was the greatest human being who ever lived (Matt. 11:11). Now that's high praise!

But circumstances didn't unfold the way John thought they would. He was thrown in prison, waiting to be executed while Jesus walked around healing other people. Why would Jesus perform miracles for strangers, but not for him? And so, John sent some of his followers to ask Jesus an astonishing question: "Are you the one who is to come [that is, the Messiah]?" (Matt. 11:3).

This is the very thing John had been boldly preaching, and now he's questioning it for himself.

I wonder if, in your own brokenness, you sometimes doubt the very truth you have committed your life to speaking. I know I have.

***Peter asked, "How can you?"***

And then there is one of Jesus' favorite disciples, Peter, chosen to be the foundational pastor of the New Testament church. Peter, who walked on water, who saw Jesus transfigured, who left everything to become a "fisher" of people. Peter, who despite his best intentions, ended up denying he even knew Jesus.

Peter's doubts were not so much about God, but about himself. In the days that followed Jesus' crucifixion and resurrection, maybe no one was more tormented than Peter. In his wrestling, he had to wonder if Jesus would take back His blessing, His calling, and His friendship. How could Jesus use a broken, unfaithful disciple who failed him when it mattered the most? In his shame and discouragement, Peter went back to fishing.

Even if you believe in the resurrected Lord, do you wonder how He can still love you? Do you think, like Peter, you are washed up, disqualified, and sidelined from God's plan?

✦ ✦ ✦

I want you to notice that in each of these four situations, a stronghold began to form. Mary and Martha teetered on a bitterness that would have hardened their hearts to Jesus' love. Paul could have doubted the power of God and even his own sanctification because of his weakness. John the Baptist, facing death, could have recanted what he had spent his short life proclaiming. And Peter was on the verge of giving up his calling, settling into a life of regret and defeat.

When they asked the questions that represented their strongholds, Jesus did not ignore or shame them. He answered with compassion, authority, and clarity:

**To Mary and Martha**, He said, "This tragedy is actually so that you may know the power of God."

**To Paul**, He said, "I want you to know that My grace is enough for you. You will experience My power more perfectly because this weakness makes you depend on Me."

**To John the Baptist**, He said, "Look at My miraculous power displayed around you! Don't be offended when My ways don't make sense to you."

**And to Peter**, Jesus said, "Remember your love for Me. Your failure does not discount that. I have commissioned you to feed My sheep."

Know that Jesus sees the stronghold your brokenness represents. He hears you when you ask the hard questions and doesn't condemn you. His words in response may not be as quick or succinct as a Bible verse, but He will answer you when you seek Him.

## YOUR JOURNEY TOWARD WHOLENESS

As it has become more acceptable in our culture (and Christian subculture) to talk about sexual struggles, you may be hearing more stories about the sexual wounds and brokenness people around you have experienced. While I am very thankful for the testimonies of Christians who share about their battles with trauma, sin, and brokenness, it seems that far too often, their stories of freedom are simplified.

I was addicted, now I don't struggle anymore.

My father abused me, but I'm all better now.

I cheated on my wife, but God completely healed our marriage.

While God does bring incredible freedom and healing, it's usually not as fast nor as complete as a thirty-minute testimony communicates. In truth, not every marriage is saved. Not everyone who battles unwanted sexual desire finds complete freedom in this lifetime. And those with healed wounds from trauma may still battle triggers and fears. Unfortunately, you are not likely to hear this truth, and so you may feel like the only Christian who seems to be wandering.

I have been beyond blessed to hear the longer, more authentic versions of what it often looks like to find healing from abuse, addiction, betrayal, and other experiences of brokenness. The journey is messy. It's grueling. It's confusing. And for most, it certainly doesn't feel like a linear path of all success and victory.

At some level, we all live in the tension between the bondage of our brokenness and God's promise of freedom and deliverance. There is no one living on planet Earth who walks in the complete fullness of the peace, joy, love, and intimacy for which God created them. We only get a foreshadow, an increasingly hopeful glimpse of what God promised us. Why? Because we are still waiting for the complete healing John described in the book of Revelation:

> Then I saw "a new heaven and a new earth," for the first heaven and the first earth had passed away, and there was no longer any sea. I saw the Holy City, the new Jerusalem, coming down out of heaven from God, prepared as a bride beautifully dressed for her husband. And I heard a loud voice from the throne saying, "Look! God's dwelling place is now among the people, and he will dwell with them. They will be his people, and God himself will be with them and be their God. 'He will wipe every tear from their eyes. There will be no more death' or mourning or crying or pain, for the old order of things has passed away." (Rev. 21:1–4)

We are waiting for heaven, but that waiting isn't just about apathetically sitting around. It involves taking steps of faith, day by day, toward God's promise to bind up the brokenhearted, free the captives, to comfort those who mourn, replacing their anguish with joy (Isa. 61:1–3). The testimonies you have heard may be messier than they seem, but they still represent the true work of God to bring healing, redemption, and freedom from brokenness.

The changes in our lives as we move from brokenness to wholeness are not all-or-nothing but happen on a continuum. As you journey toward wholeness, there may be seasons when you feel like you are making no progress at all. It's common to relapse into old patterns, to be triggered by fears, to get angry long after you've decided to forgive, and to return to doubts you thought you buried a long time ago. Because of this, we can feel like nothing is happening. Many times I've heard people on the journey of healing say things like, "I can't believe I'm back here again. I thought all of this was dealt with and settled." But even in seasons of feeling stuck, God can be moving, unearthing those strongholds in order to do a deeper work of healing and redemption. If that describes where you are, don't give up hope. Keep pursuing the Lord and wholeness. Even if it sometimes feels like you are going through the motions, God is working in the unseen, spiritual world.

One woman, Sondra, described her long journey of healing through our online book studies:

> I am finishing up my seventh time reading *God, Sex, and Your Marriage*[6] (my book is falling apart)! Every time I have read through this book, I would physically shake and could hear my heartbeat in my head. I have struggled every day that I knew our online book study group was to meet with headaches, fear, attacks but also excitement with what God would do in me and in the group. There has been so much healing for

me through this book and every time it's something different and it's been an emotional ride.

This time through has been a different experience for me, last night I realized why. I can finally say I have a very healthy marriage with a good sex life. I can finally see sex as a gift whereas before that idea made me sick to my stomach. . . . I finally get it! God has transformed me spiritually and mentally around this area. I can now fully minister to others around this subject without the roller coaster of my own issues.

These past four years that I've been in nonstop online book study groups and seeking healing, I now have a new definition of what God's church can be.

I'm overwhelmed by Sondra's tenacity and commitment to healing!

The Bible describes wholeness in Christ using the metaphor of fruit. I'm not a gardener, but I know that fruit doesn't magically appear in a moment. It takes years of tilling, fertilizing, sunshine, and rain. And that fruit that was so evident in summer is totally gone in the dead of winter. Even when the fruit disappears, the tree is preparing for a greater harvest in the next season. The same is true as you surrender your brokenness to the Lord.

You might not always see it in yourself, but over the months and years as you surrender your sexuality to the Lord, there will be shifts that become obvious in your life.

The Holy Spirit doesn't invade every nook and cranny of your life all at once. He intercedes for you, gently taking back ground piece by piece. This is a progressive journey of freedom. There are so many men and women on this same journey of freedom. Sondra is one of them.

At one level, we can't see the end of our own stories, but we do know that God never wastes our pain. As you heal, you will probably still have questions about why God allows so much pain, but you will also become amazed by His capacity to redeem your pain. We find this promise in

Romans 8:28: "And we know that in all things God works for the good of those who love him, who have been called according to his purpose." That might feel like shallow comfort as you wade through days of depression, anxiety, and overwhelming shame. How could God use that betrayal, that horrible abuse, the years of bondage for your good?

I've known Ginger for many years. She is the victim of horrendous physical, sexual, and emotional abuse from childhood. In the wake of her pain, Ginger's life as a young adult was chaotic, filled with promiscuity, alcohol, and drugs. Ginger has been on the journey of healing and surrender for more than forty years. She would tell you that there have been seasons of discouragement and deep pain, along with seasons of great victory.

> ***Remember that Satan's aim is to keep you from the goodness of God.***

Ginger is one of the most powerful witnesses to God's love and grace that I know. Every year, she leads a small group through our ministry that ends up transforming lives. Because of her wounds, she has gone deeper in the journey of knowing Jesus than most Christians would dare. Ginger's wounds have become her greatest weapons against the enemy. She comforts others with the comfort she has received. She encourages others with the freedom that she is experiencing.

As her friend, I wish Ginger had never experienced the horrors of her childhood. But I see God working all things in her life for His glory and for Ginger's good. Now we see just a glimpse of the ways Ginger's brokenness has been turned against the enemy. I can only imagine what it will be like when she sees her Savior face-to-face.

I think of others I've been privileged to know. Couples who have battled through betrayal and sexual addiction to help others find the freedom they now know. I think of men and women whose marriages weren't saved, but their personal brokenness was redeemed as they learned to know Jesus as their strength, their confidence, and their Beloved.

Remember that Satan's aim is not to destroy your sex life, but to keep you from the goodness of God. Surrendering your brokenness is not just about asking God to take away the problems in your life, but for Him to show up in the midst of them. Sometimes we don't recognize how we are healing because our *circumstances* may not be changing. Instead, God is at work within, changing *us*.

## WHAT WE NEED TO HEAL

While our brokenness has an undercurrent of spiritual warfare, this does not negate the very real physical, relational, and psychological realities of our wounds. We don't just "pray" our way out of the effects of trauma or recite Bible verses in the wake of a spouse's betrayal.

I'm often asked what I think about counseling. Do you *need* a therapist to find healing?

I am trained as a clinical psychologist and understand the benefits of the knowledge we have gleaned over the past several decades. But I also realize that not everyone has access to professional counseling.

Whether or not you can go to counseling, here are four elements that can propel you on your journey of surrendered brokenness. Sometimes God provides these healing agents through a therapist, but God is always extending us the invitation to healing and redemption in our brokenness.

### *1. We need a safe place to tell the truth*

A key part of healing is the opportunity to talk openly about what happened to us. Trauma is "a person's experience of emotional distress resulting from an event that overwhelms the capacity to emotionally digest it."[7] Sexual traumas can include sexual violence, harassment, intimate partner betrayal, and early exposure to pornography.

By its very nature, trauma is something that doesn't get integrated into your life and conscious awareness. And so it gets sidelined, compartmentalized, and in some situations, completely forgotten. Your brain responds to this experience storing traumatic memories in the amygdala area of your brain, rather than being processed as normal experiences are by the prefrontal cortex and stored in the hippocampus. "The amygdala stores the visual images of trauma as sensory fragments, which means the trauma memory is not stored like a story, rather by how our five senses were experiencing the trauma at the time it was occurring. The memories are stored through fragments of visual images, smells, sounds, tastes, or touch."[8] This is why sexual wounds can result in being triggered by touch or smell, even if you struggle to put words to the memory.

In the course of typical daily life, you don't have many places to talk about sexual wounds. Unfortunately, sexual trauma often happens within a close relational context like a family or church community. How do you talk about sexual wounding when it may result in "your word against theirs" or threaten to create massive conflict among the people you care about?

We also don't talk about our sexual brokenness because we often feel the shame of being somehow responsible for what happened to us. And so we soldier on with life with no place to process events that have deeply impacted our understanding of sex, of our bodies and desires, and of the goodness of God.

***I have never met someone who healed while keeping their pain a secret.***

Even most people who go to counseling typically seek help for symptoms like relational problems, anxiety, or sexual dysfunction. Many are completely unaware of how their past trauma plays into their current difficulty.

Healing requires a safe space not only to talk about what happened to us, but to be honest with how we are processing it. For many people, counseling is the best first step in healing because it is naturally designed to be a safe place to talk about sensitive personal experiences. Counselors are bound by law to keep conversations confidential, with certain exceptions. You also assume your counselor has heard it all and won't judge you. A therapist might use techniques like EMDR therapy (eye movement desensitization and reprocessing), art therapy, or somatic therapy to help you access and express memories and feelings that are difficult to process.

> ***The Word of God and a biblical community are so important. We can't feel our way to truth. We need to be rooted in it.***

Not every counselor is the right fit, and you might find a safe place to process wounds with a trusted friend, mentor, or within a supportive community designed for transparency and vulnerability.

Regardless of the source, you need a safe place to be truly known and understood. I have never met someone who healed while keeping their pain a secret. As difficult as it may feel to take that first step, you can't heal in hiding.

***2. We need a trustworthy source to find truth***

By their very nature, wounds are disorienting. Our thinking and feelings can become so distorted that we can't discern which way is up. Jesus said that Satan, our enemy, is the father of all lies. He actually can't speak the truth, because lying is his native language. In your wounds, Satan whispers disorienting lies like:

You deserve the pain you experienced.
No one would love you if they knew what you have done.
You can't trust anyone.
Men only want one thing.

Your healing requires that you identify and confront lies with what is true. Jesus claimed "I am the way and the truth and the life" (John 14:6). He doesn't just speak truth, He IS truth!

Sometimes a caring therapist or supportive friend might be encouraging but may not be a great source of truth. Modern psychology is largely rooted in postmodern thought, encouraging you to heal yourself with positive thoughts that aren't necessarily based on truth. In *Rid of My Disgrace*, Justin and Lindsay Holcomb explain:

> In an attempt to counter your negative self-image, others may encourage you to see yourself in a story of self-love, self-reliance, and self-healing. But the identity that comes from that story is even darker disgrace and even more pain in the longer term because the self-made illusions about self cannot be maintained.[9]

This is where the Word of God and a biblical community become so important. We can't feel our way to truth. We need to be rooted in it, abiding in Christ as the trustworthy anchor of our lives.

### 3. *We need a healthy community in which to integrate truth*

*"My name is Bob, and I'm an alcoholic."*

*"Hello, Bob."*

This is the well-known phrase everyone is asked to use when they introduce themselves at an AA meeting. Have you ever wondered why? Doesn't this introduction label people as helpless in a shameful addiction?

As I mentioned, our wounds and struggles are often compartmentalized. You might appear to the people who know you as competent, kind, and put-together. Over the years, you've probably worked hard to keep the ugliness of your brokenness from seeping into your relationships and daily life.

Let's say you take that first step and share your brokenness with a counselor or trusted friend, but few others in your life have any idea of what you are walking through. And so in the protected space of one or two relationships, you can be real and truly known. But everywhere else you go, you can only present the "acceptable you."

The Bible calls the church the "body of Christ." Within that body, He has placed spiritual gifts and personalities who are meant to minister to you. Through His Spirit, they are ready to welcome the real truth about you and show you in tangible ways God's kindness, compassion, generosity, wisdom, and grace. But they can't do that if you keep hiding.

What happens in the counseling room or while you are doing your personal devotions needs to be integrated into what it means to be you. How does your past abuse impact how you feel around men? Around women? With your spouse? How do you learn healthier ways of relating without being around people who will love you and care for you on the healing journey?

Psychiatrist Dr. Curt Thompson is regarded in the Christian community as a leading expert in helping people overcome brokenness and shame. Curt's research and practice have led him to the conclusion that the most essential ingredient to healing is a community that helps us integrate our brokenness into the realities and narrative of our lives. He writes, "We are all born into the world looking for someone looking for us, and we remain in this mode of searching for the rest of our lives. At the deepest levels of what it means to be human, we long for connection in order for us to thrive, both individually and collectively."[10]

Unfortunately, most of us don't know how to find that kind of vulnerable, caring community. You might start by connecting with a Christian ministry like Authentic Intimacy, Pure Desire, Celebrate Recovery, or Curt Thompson's ministry, Confessional Communities, that intentionally create spaces for people to seek the Lord's healing and love together.

### *4. We need a relationship with the One who is Truth*

The safe space to share, the Bible to remind you of truth, the community that embodies grace—these are essential elements of your healing journey, but each one points to the most important thing: encountering the Healer Himself.

A counselor can help, but only the Healer can heal.

There have been a few seasons in my life where I needed help to heal. The Lord brought some wise and gifted people to show me God's kindness and wisdom, and to help me understand how my brokenness was keeping me stuck. In the moment, that person usually became like a "savior" to me. I hung on every word and treasured the time I had in their presence. Eventually, each of those relationships needed to fade, sometimes in a way that was painful, for me to recognize that only Jesus can be my true Healer and Savior. Every other person, no matter how loving and helpful they were, would eventually disappoint or leave. I had to learn that this was not abandonment, but Jesus' way of transferring my ultimate dependence to Him. The best of His people must ultimately point to the Healer Himself, the One who will never leave me nor forsake me.

> ***Ask Him your hard questions. Pour out your anguish. And then fall into His open arms as He says to you, "Come to me."***

Surrendering your brokenness happens when God not only breaks the stronghold but He becomes your stronghold. You no longer hide *from* Him, but you run to hide *in* Him. David wrote in Psalm 121:1–2, "I lift up my eyes to the mountains—where does my help come from? My help comes from the Lord, the Maker of heaven and earth."

God is not a distant being who feels pity for us in our brokenness. He demonstrated His great love for us by taking on human flesh, enduring the scorn and rejection of men. He was betrayed, abused, stripped naked, all in front of a mocking crowd. Through His suffering, Jesus entered the stronghold of every human wound. As a result, "This High Priest of ours understands our weaknesses, faced all of the same testings we do, yet he did not sin. So let us come boldly to the throne of our gracious God. There we will receive his mercy, and we will find grace to help us when we need it most" (Heb. 4:15–16 NLT).

Jesus doesn't ask you to surrender your sexuality or anything else without opening His arms wide to you. Pound on heaven's door for relief. Ask Him your hard questions. Pour out your anguish. And then fall into His open arms as He says to you, "Come to me, you who are weary and burdened, and I will give you rest. Take my yoke upon you and learn from me, for I am gentle and humble in heart, and you will find rest for your souls" (Matt. 11:28–29).

## Application Exercise:

---

This chapter addressed four questions that lead to strongholds in our relationship with God. Which of these four questions have you asked in response to sexual brokenness?

God, where were You?
God, why don't You?
Are You really God?
God, how could You?

What are the events in your life that have led you to ask that question?

How does that question represent a barrier in your relationship with God today?

This chapter mentions four things you need on the journey of healing. Identify which of these four you are currently experiencing and which you are lacking.

1. Safe space
2. Source of truth
3. Healthy community
4. Relationship with Jesus

What is a step you can take toward the one(s) you may be lacking?

## Passages to Study:

***Read the prophecy of Jesus' suffering recorded in Isaiah 53.***

Which of the things Jesus suffered can you personally identify with?

How does it affect your understanding of Jesus to know He suffered these things for us?

How can we come to know Jesus through our own suffering, rejection, and grief?

***Read Psalm 34.***

In what ways was David suffering when he wrote this psalm? (See 1 Sam. 21:10–22:1.)

What promises are in this psalm?

What promise can you cling to today in your brokenness?

## Questions for personal reflection and discussion:

---

1. Why do you think it is so much more common to talk about how God wants us to change our behavior than it is to encourage people to surrender their wounds?
2. Why do you think sexual brokenness sets up the potential for spiritual strongholds that keep us from knowing God?
3. Do you think Christians tend to oversimplify the journey of healing? If so, what can be the result of that?
5. What is the danger of having supportive people in your life but no trustworthy source of truth?
6. What is the danger of having a trustworthy source of truth in your life, but no safe space or community to process your brokenness?
7. Why is it essential that we ultimately bring our brokenness to Jesus and not only rely on other people?

CHAPTER 6

# Surrendered Idols

I was a twenty-year-old college student; it was Saturday night. My roommate and friends all seemed to have plans (dates!), but I had none. Sometimes I dreaded the weekends because they highlighted my loneliness. This was the time of my life that should have been filled with fun, love, and dating. What was wrong with me?

Then I was thirty-five, married with three young children. I no longer sat bored and lonely on Saturday nights. Now I complained about being exhausted—everyone seemed to want more of me. Although my husband was always physically with me, we had conflicts that made us feel distant. Instead of romantic and sexual pleasure, marriage felt more like a season of *Survivor*. I had the things I had once longed for, but still felt empty, lonely, and frustrated with my unfulfilled desires.

The apostle Paul wrote that he had learned how to be content in all circumstances (Phil. 4:12). I think I had learned how to be *discontent* in all circumstances!

## "IF ONLY" IDOLS

The late Tim Keller wrote *Counterfeit Gods*, a convicting book in which he explains how God's good gifts (like sex and marriage) can become idols in our hearts. "We think that idols are bad things, but that is almost never the case. . . . The greater the good, the more likely we are to expect that it can satisfy our deepest needs and hopes. What is an idol? It is anything more important to you than God, anything that absorbs your heart and imagination more than God, anything you seek to give you what only God can give you."[1]

Often, our hidden idols are revealed through the thought that begins with "if only . . ."

If only I could find "the one" . . .

If only God would let me be with who I love . . .

If only my wife would have sex with me . . .

If only I was married to a man who cared about me . . .

If only I could feel normal . . .

Much of our own sexual sin, disappointment, and struggle is tied up in hanging on to our "if onlys" as idols.

What is your "if only"?

## MAKING GOOD GIFTS IDOLS

The gifts of sexual pleasure, romantic attachment, and marriage are beautiful expressions of God's goodness and love to us. However, they become idols when we look to them to meet our deepest needs and to fix what feels so broken within us. God's will for us is to honor the gifts of sexuality and marriage without worshiping them. We live in a culture that does the exact opposite. Sexual fulfillment and romantic attachment are worshiped as essential to human happiness, but not honored as God's creation.

Instead of challenging the culture's worship of sex and romance, we have too often Christianized it. Author Dani Treweek, whose ministry is focused on the gift of singleness, observes, "Where romantic love is considered to be necessary for genuine human fulfillment then, logically speaking, marriage—the legitimate arena in which romantic love might be permanently enacted among Christians—also becomes necessary for human happiness."[2]

Sometimes the church unintentionally feeds into the idolatry of marriage and sex. In fact, so much of our church culture is built around the centrality of marriage that singles often feel like they don't belong. For example, churches sometimes gear the majority of their programming around marriage and children. It becomes far more difficult to surrender your longings for marriage and sex when the church reinforces it as a cure-all.

And singleness itself can become an idol. Some Christians are so afraid of losing their independence, they are not even open to marriage. Committing to another person and having children threaten their idols of achievement, independence, and a comfortable life.

Whether or not you are married, having the right perspective of marriage and sexuality is critical for you to honor it. It is impossible to honor the gifts of sex and marriage while also worshiping them. Only when we let go of something as an idol can we value it in the proper place. Wrong beliefs about the holiness and purpose of these gifts can be one of the bonds that keeps you tied to sexual sin; it can also be the foundation of the barrier in your relationship with God.

✦ ✦ ✦

We have become so influenced by unhealthy perspectives about marriage and sexuality that it can help to remember some basic biblical truths about the priority and beauty of these gifts. Let's look at them from a kingdom perspective.

***Sex and marriage are good gifts***

Even though we live in a broken and sinful world, we can still enjoy the very good gifts of marriage, sex, children, and male/female relationships.

You may be so jaded by your experience of dating, sex, or marriage that you have forgotten the goodness of these gifts. Unfortunately, more young adults are forgoing marriage, choosing instead to live together or stay unattached.

God created us with needs for intimacy, belonging, and significance. His created structure of the family is a good gift not only to individuals, but to society as a whole. There is nothing wrong with desiring and pursuing marriage. It is a good thing (Prov. 18:22; 1 Cor. 7). We are all to honor marriage by thinking of it as a blessing and encouraging those who are married to value it as such.

Way back in Genesis 2, before sin entered the world, God created Adam and then Eve. These two humans, made in the image of God, were both similar and different from each other. We also read that they were "naked and felt no shame" and that they enjoyed the first marriage, including sex. Within the perfection of God's exquisite garden, we see male, female, nakedness, sex, and the covenant of marriage. God created this union to be life-giving and reproductive, and Genesis 1:31 says that God saw all this as "very good"!

### *Seek God's kingdom first*

Good things can become "god things," which is what sometimes happens with marriage and sex. A good thing is something you would like to have. A god thing is something you *must* have.

Tim Keller explains how the root of sexual sin is not that sexual desire is bad, but that it becomes a greater drive than our desire for God:

> The word that the NIV translates "sinful desires" and the ESV [English Standard Version] renders "lusts" is *epithumia*. Literally, it means "over-desire" an all-controlling drive and longing. This is revealing. The main problem of our heart is not so much desires for bad things, but our over-desires for good things, our turning of created, good things

> into gods, objects of our worship and service. And the worst thing that can happen to us is that we are given what our hearts over-desire.[3]

***When marriage, sexual fulfillment, or having a family become the key to what we think will make us happy, they will become a source of pain rather than blessing.***

Jesus' ministry redefined priorities for a Christian, teaching that *everything* must be secondary to our pursuit of God and His kingdom (Matt. 6:33). Jesus went so far as to say if we love our family members (including the potential of a family) more than we love God, we are not worthy of Him (Matt. 10:37). Our family relationships matter. In other places, the Bible tells us to take care of our parents, our children, and our spouse. Jesus' point is that every other relationship must be secondary to our trust in God and commitment to His kingdom.

When marriage, sexual fulfillment, or having a family become the key to what we think will make us happy, they will become a source of pain rather than blessing. A longing never satisfied. A spouse you cannot change. A love that always seems just out of reach. A dream God seems to be keeping from you.

Jesus taught that there will be no marriage in heaven, meaning that marriage is lifelong but not eternal (Matt. 22:30). God created marriage and sex to be a holy, earthbound metaphor of His covenant love; they are temporary good gifts to point to our eternal relationship with God. You were not married when you were born, and you won't be married after you die. You won't need the metaphor of marriage and sex once you are in the reality of our eternal covenant with God.

This is convicting not just for the single Christian who longs to be married, but also for the married Christian who becomes obsessed with *happily ever after*. God did not create marriage so that a husband and wife would live facing each other at all times, but so that they could be side by side in their journey as fellow Christians.

My husband is not my Savior. He is not my future. He is not my purpose in life. I can most fully enjoy the good gift of marriage when I receive it in context of the greater gift and greater call of the One who loves me and gave Himself for me (Gal. 2:20).

### *Singleness is also a gift*

The apostle Paul who wrote about marriage and sex as a mystery pointing to Christ and the church was a single man. Instead of looking for a wife or pining away in loneliness, Paul was thankful to be single. In fact, he wrote, "I wish you were all single like I am." (See 1 Cor. 7:7.)

Why would he write that?

Paul had an unshakable intimacy with God through Jesus. He was absolutely, 100 percent committed to the kingdom of God. In his letters to the early Christians, he wanted them to have this same passion for knowing and serving the Lord. They lived in an ancient world that was much like our own, surrounded by sexual temptations and sensuality. He saw these early Christians distracted by the pursuit of marriage and sexual pleasure and wanted them to be free from these obsessions.

Paul's overriding teaching in 1 Corinthians 7 and elsewhere is that marriage can refine our understanding of love and stewardship of our sexuality, but it also can be a distraction in our relationship with God and work in His kingdom. "Those who are married are concerned about many things. Their interests are divided between working on their marriage and serving God. When you are single, you can be completely available to how God leads you" (paraphrase of 1 Cor. 7).

Singleness provides more flexibility with time and money to say yes to friendships, travel, and ultimately Christian priorities. I have several single friends (male and female), who are thriving in their relationship with God and their ministry lives. Laurence is one of them. He shares:

> The gift of singleness is not for me to just do whatever I want, but to give myself fully and unconditionally to not one person in particular (like marriage), but to multiple people, to the community. It teaches me to love self-sacrificially, while it delivers me from my selfishness, when I commit myself to the family of God, who I am related to by His blood. To love more like Jesus loved, that is to me the origin of our "thriving," doesn't matter if we are married or single. Because I believe we are ultimately made for that, to love like Him. And I have experienced the deep joy of that in the midst of unfulfilled longings, loneliness, and hurt.

Yes, there are real losses with lifelong singleness, but there are also unique challenges and pain points in marriage that single Christians don't have to deal with. Whether single or married, life will have disappointments and heartache. Life can also have joy, significance, and deep intimacy regardless of your marital status.

You were created for intimacy with God and with His people. Your sexual desires will fade with time, but you will never outgrow your need for intimacy. You need intimacy with God, but you also need family, especially the family of God.

Some singles understand covenant more profoundly than married Christians because they have skipped the metaphor of marriage and are more invested in the ultimate covenant of intimacy with Christ. Christopher West explains, "Celibacy for the kingdom *is not a rejection of sexuality*. It's a call to embrace *the ultimate meaning and purpose of sexuality*. The 'one flesh' union is only a foreshadowing of something infinitely more glorious."[4]

Bree shares how this truth has helped her understand the gift of singleness:

> The deepest desire of my heart has always been to be intimately known and loved. Growing up in purity culture, when I heard "save sex for marriage," I thought that meant "save all intimacy for marriage." So I built a wall between myself and everyone else, including God, and put all my hope in a future husband. He would meet all my needs for intimacy, redeem me from the shame I felt about my sexuality, and we would live happily ever after. That husband never came.
>
> God began to show me that the husband I was longing for was real. Not an earthly husband and temporary marriage, but a heavenly bridegroom that invited me into an eternal covenant with Him and His people. He taught me what real intimacy is and how to cultivate it. He showed me the true purpose of my sexuality, that it's meant to draw me into intimacy, not just sex, and redeem me from my shame. Jesus stepped into my story and invited me into His, one where I can build deep, intimate relationships here and now, with Him and His people, that will last into eternity.

Unfortunately, our contemporary church culture has defined marriage not as an optional gift from God, but as an essential part of being a mature Christian adult.[5] This belief puts an extraordinary pressure on marriage and causes single Christians to feel as if they are deficient, abnormal, and unqualified for positions of leadership in the church. For example, a young man recently told me that he offered to host a small group in his home, but his church elders told him that only married couples were allowed to do so. Your marital status is not what qualifies you for service to God, spiritual maturity, or a fulfilled life in Christ.

### *Is sex a need?*

It's interesting to me that we teach single Christians that they can live without sex, but once someone gets married, we begin to frame it as an absolute requirement for survival. Sex can be a very pressing desire and longing. In some seasons of life, it may feel like a need—as necessary as food and water. But no one has ever died from not having sex.

I love how therapist and author Sam Jolman helps men distinguish between a drive and a desire:

> Sex is a desire, not a drive. It's a want, not a need. Calling sex a "drive" isn't just bumbled wording. It encourages us men to treat sex as a need, something akin to life and death, which confuses our relationship with our bodies. Men get stuck relating to sexuality as a necessity, an urge they have to answer, something they are powerless to stop. This perspective keeps men from having a conversation with their bodies and sexuality, and puts them in survival-reaction mode.[6]

C. S. Lewis wrote about this dynamic in his classic book *Mere Christianity*: "Our warped natures, the devils who tempt us, and all the contemporary propaganda for lust, combine to make us feel that the desires we are resisting are so 'natural,' so 'healthy,' and so reasonable, that it is almost perverse and abnormal to resist them."[7]

We make sex a *need* when it becomes our way of coping with life. In essence, this is the definition of a sexual addiction. Sex (or pornography or masturbation) becomes your "drug" to manage depression, loneliness, anxiety, or boredom.

God created sex to be pleasurable for a couple as a gift in marriage. Even through seasons of difficulty, sex can help reconnect and bond a husband and wife. But when you use sex to cope with loneliness or other difficult life experiences, it works like a drug. You rely on porn, masturbation, or other sexual releases to make it through the day. This can happen to someone who is single or married.

If sex has become something that feels like a need (essential to your well-being), you are using God's good gift in a way that has enslaved you to physical pleasure. If this describes you, you are not alone! There are a number of amazing ministries and resources to help you pursue health in your brain chemistry, thoughts, and relationships.[8]

Marriage is one way to honor God with our sexuality, providing the opportunity for our sexual desires to be channeled and refined in covenant love. Paul says that this is a valid reason to get married, but marriage is not primarily for a sexual outlet. Remember that the overriding goal for all Christians is to glorify God with our bodies. Both the married and single Christian have that call.

For single Christians, that means a commitment to no sex, which obviously requires a lot of self-control. But for the married Christian, discipline is also required to "live a life filled with love" (Eph. 5:2 NLT) within your sexual relationship. It's not a free-for-all, each spouse thinking, *I should get all my needs met.*

As you learned from Paul in 1 Corinthians, a Christian's body no longer belongs just to themselves but also to God. Paul adds to that principle for married Christians. Their bodies belong to self, to God, *and* to their spouse (1 Cor. 7:3–4). As a married Christian woman, I don't make sexual decisions alone, but I yield my body first to God, and then to my husband (he does the same to me). We belong to each other and aim to honor each other in our sexuality.

Your spouse is not an acceptable outlet for your sexual lust, nor is he or she your safeguard against sexual sin. Self-control—sexual or otherwise—is the fruit of the Holy Spirit's work as you surrender your life to God (Gal. 5:22–24). Your spouse is God's son or daughter, whom you are called to love as He loves.

### *The family of God is primary*

A few months ago, I was talking with a Christian woman who had been widowed for several years. She had just reentered the dating scene. When

I asked her what she was hoping for in a dating relationship, she said, "I don't think I want to get married again. I just feel lonely. Juli, we live in a couples' world, and I feel like I don't belong without a significant other."

**If you are blessed to have a husband, child, mother, or father, thank God for these gifts. But don't let these blessings crowd out your primary family—the family of God.**

My friend put into words what many single, divorced, and widowed Christians experience. Their need is not for marriage or sex per se, but their need is to belong, to be seen and to be connected.

The most important interpersonal relationship in Christianity is not husband and wife but being part of the family of God. In her book *No Greater Love*, Rebecca McLaughlin points out how we have elevated marriage in a way that Jesus never intended. "For Christians, family does come first. But it's the family of faith, not of biology."[9] Rebecca explains how we've messed this up. We think marriage is essential and friendship is optional. Instead, Jesus taught that friendship is essential, but marriage is optional.

If you are blessed to have a husband, child, mother, or father, thank God for these gifts. But don't let these blessings crowd out your primary family—the family of God. As Christians, we must be invested in the family of God within our local communities and churches. Jesus modeled this when His mother and brothers were trying to get His attention as He was teaching. He responded,

> "Who is my mother, and who are my brothers?" Pointing to his disciples, he said, "Here are my mother and my brothers. For whoever does the will of my Father in heaven is my brother and sister and mother." (Matt. 12:48–50)

It is noteworthy that God gives us the language of "brother and sister" in how we relate to each other. I have two brothers and three sisters. I know how to have a shared history, deep friendship, and great affection for my siblings without any shred of romance or sexualization. That is the template from which God wants us to navigate our Christian relationships. This is not only possible, but essential for how God designed the church to function.

Unfortunately, many of us, whether single or married, don't know how to develop the kind of friendships and community that create that deep sense of belonging. Significant friendships both within same sex and opposite sex relationships can become complicated, with blurred boundaries and confusing feelings. While there are many books on healthy marriages, there are few that help us understand how to develop healthy friendships. Interestingly, the Bible has far more to say on how to be a friend (a brother or sister in Christ) than it says on how to be a husband or wife. If you are married, your relationship with your spouse is first one of brother or sister in the Lord. That primary relationship doesn't change when you say, "I do." It just has an added layer to it.

In recent years, a number of thoughtful Christian leaders have been writing and teaching on this topic, helping the church return to the biblical priority of God's family.[10] I'd encourage you to thoughtfully engage with this kind of content, but in the meantime, here are some highlights:

**Not all attraction or intimacy is sexual.** Many Christians are leery of forming anything more than a superficial relationship with other believers. They are understandably concerned about sexual attraction and maintaining boundaries. Unfortunately, everything seems to be sexualized in our current relational climate, including same-sex friendships. God has given you the capacity to feel deeply attached to and drawn to many different people. Most of those relationships were never meant to be sexualized but enjoyed as a gift revealing different aspects of God's character. However, remember that only marriage is exclusive. If you find yourself feeling possessive or jealous in a friendship, that is a sign that it has become unhealthy. You need significant friendships within the Christian community that are informed by God's truth. Don't be shy about seeking wisdom from a counselor or mentor if you see signs of blurred boundaries or codependency in a friendship.

**The family of God is essential to an enduring commitment to sexual integrity.** My friends Zack and Kate lead a church ministry to same-sex attracted seekers and believers. They share how essential the family of God is to those who surrender their sexuality for the sake of Christ:

> A biological family seems to not be in the future of many of those who come to our ministry. Again and again, we hear the deep pain of loneliness and unmet longings for intimacy—and for some these painful experiences have caused them to reject God's design for marriage. The loneliness and isolation is just too deep. The question these same-sex attracted believers are facing is whether it's better to disobey God to have an earthly expression of family with someone of the same sex or to live a life of loneliness. God has designed the church to be the answer. As our church learns to operate as a family, we offer these brothers and sisters a pathway for obedience, belonging, and a flourishing life. Though this doesn't mean a life without loneliness, it does offer rich relationships with brothers and sisters where they can be deeply known, loved, and know that they belong.

Over years of ministry, I have learned that this is not only essential to same-sex attracted Christians, but also to those who are single, widowed, divorced, or isolated within marriage. Psalm 68:6 says, "God sets the lonely in families." We were meant to be that family.

## CONTENTMENT: THE ANTIDOTE FOR IDOLATRY

What idol is God revealing in your heart as you read through this chapter? How have you turned God's good gifts into something you must have to be happy?

I wonder how much our struggles with sexuality are rooted in a lack of contentment. Whether you are single or married, you want something more than what you have. My friend Jake says it clearly:

> I have always wanted to love and be loved. A painful breakup followed by years of being single has led me to question God's goodness and trustworthiness. I know God loves me and that He will provide for me, but loneliness and unanswered prayers for a partner cause me to feel abandoned and neglected by God. I have grown somewhat angry, bitter, and doubtful, particularly as I watch my friends and cousins find their soulmates one by one while I remain alone. How do I maintain joy and trust God when my need for companionship is continually unmet?

Regardless of what your idols may be, contentment is the antidote. If we are not content in our current situation, we will end up using good gifts like sex and marriage for our own purposes instead of for God's. We will sacrifice our call to be part of the kingdom of God and invest in His family because we will be obsessed by the thing that we think will bring happiness.

As I mentioned, Paul addressed the importance of contentment in his letter to the Philippian church. He was writing about money and material comforts, but his wisdom can help us pursue contentment in every area of our lives. Because Paul was content in Jesus, he wasn't destroyed either by having great blessing nor by what he was lacking.

> I know what it is to be in need, and I know what it is to have plenty. I have learned the secret of being content in any and every situation, whether well fed or hungry, whether living in plenty or in want. I can do all this through him who gives me strength. (Phil. 4:12–13)

I find it reassuring that Paul said contentment was something he needed to *learn* because it certainly doesn't come naturally to me! Even when things are going well, I can focus on what I am missing rather than the good gifts God has given. Paul had to develop the capacity for contentment over time, and so can we.

God has something to teach us about contentment in every season of life, not just when we experience loss or frustration. Seasons of blessing teach us contentment because we realize that God's gifts are wonderful, but also not able to satisfy us. Maybe you finally got married only to find that it didn't solve your loneliness problem. Seasons of trials teach us contentment because we realize that, although we might be suffering, we are still surviving. Often, we experience God's presence, grace, and goodness more deeply through the times when we are hurting. Trials usually strip us of the things (or people) we think we need to be happy, prompting us to seek God in more intentional ways. In fact, Paul confides in another book that God's strength and grace was even greater in his weaknesses than when things were going well (2 Cor. 12:8–10).

Blessings and trials won't teach you contentment in and of themselves. Blessings can easily become idols and trials can cause us to doubt God instead of trusting Him. Paul's secret to contentment was his absolute dependence on Jesus whatever his circumstances. "I can do everything through Christ, who gives me strength" (Phil. 4:13 NLT). With Him, we can do all things. Without Him, we can do nothing.

***Contentment's eternal perspective***

I was recently in a friend's office and noticed a beautiful family picture of his daughter's wedding on his mantel. When I asked him about it, he said, "It's my favorite photo." He went on to describe the look in his wife's eyes and each of their grown children. Then he added, "Looking at this reminds me of the importance of faithfulness and endurance. We wouldn't have that picture if we had given up when things were rough."

When my friend looks at this family portrait, it reminds him of how much he has learned to value faithfulness and endurance. As we grow to know Jesus, we also become more convinced that the trials and disappointments of this world are nothing compared to what God has prepared for us in eternity. And we won't just have a beautiful family picture to remind us of this—one day we will see Jesus face-to-face.

> ***Remember, we are living not for pleasure and happiness today, but for the long-term blessing of His presence and for our eternal inheritance.***

One of my favorite Bible passages is Hebrews 11, what some people refer to as the "Hall of Faith." It recounts a list of biblical heroes who made choices based on their faith in God though, like any of us, they were imperfect. But what set these men and women apart was their eternal perspective: "They were foreigners and strangers on earth. . . . They were longing for a better country—a heavenly one. Therefore God is not ashamed to be called their God, for he has prepared a city for them" (Heb. 11:13–16).

In other words, they had faith that they were living for more than just this world. We cannot ultimately say no to the lure of idols unless we place our faith on the belief that there is more to life than this world.

Some people try to motivate Christians to live holy lives, telling them that things will go better for them on earth. Yes, that may be true. Stewarding your sexuality according to God's design may result in wonderful blessings during your earthly life. But being a follower of Jesus doesn't put your ultimate hope in this world. Our relationship with Jesus helps us remember that we are living not for pleasure and happiness today, but for the long-term blessing of His presence and for our eternal inheritance.

Most Christians talk little about eternity, but the Bible tells us to store up treasures in heaven rather than living our lives to experience short-term pleasure. The only way we can let go of the "if onlys" in our lives is to know Jesus in such a way that we truly believe that He is coming back to take us home and that the eternal rewards for our obedience will far outweigh our temporary, earthbound sacrifices.

God gives us gifts in this life for us to enjoy. We need to be sure that those gifts—or the desire for them—don't compete with our faith in what God has promised.

## LEARNING CONTENTMENT

I'm sure you would love to experience so much contentment in God that you no longer struggle with your idols. The idea of contentment is attractive, but the road to actually experience it isn't always so clear. Someone once famously prayed, "Lord, give me patience. And give it to me right now!" Maybe that's how you feel with contentment.

While we can ask God to make us content, there are also some practical things we can do to foster it in our hearts.

### *Acknowledge and grieve what isn't*

I love that the Bible doesn't present us with perfect role models, but with real people who struggled with genuine losses and longings. We see in their prayers and actions gut-wrenching pain because of what their lives lacked.

Hannah poured out her heart to God when she couldn't have a baby.
Naomi said "Call me Mara [bitter]" because she had lost her husband and sons.
David lost his family relationships, his best friend, was betrayed by his son, and was pursued by enemies.
Tamar lived with the shame and isolation of being a victim of incest.
Paul experienced discouragement, despair, and rejection.
Many psalmists wrote heartfelt poems and psalms pouring out their grief and disappointment.

These were not "crybabies," and God never told them just to get over it. The Bible tells us that God is near to the brokenhearted (Ps. 34:18). Jesus demonstrated this to us when He wept while grieving with Mary after her brother died (John 11:33–36).

There is genuine pain and grief represented in the longings God is asking you to surrender. It may be that what you hoped for wasn't just withheld but absolutely smashed.

It's okay and even part of the surrender process to name those losses, to grieve them, and to ask God the hard questions like *Where were You?* and *Why don't You?*

Surrendering our "if onlys" is so precious to God because He knows what it costs us to choose Him instead of the things we have set our hearts on.

Have you ever taken the time to acknowledge and grieve your losses?

***Appreciate and steward what is***

The human brain tends to find what it is looking for. When we feel discontent, we become hyperaware of what is missing and also tend to notice the blessings other people seem to have. When we are content, the opposite is true—we become aware of what we have and feel compassion for people who are struggling.

Most of us wait around for our circumstances to change with the hope of contentment instead of adjusting our perspective while pursuing contentment. Mental health research continues to show that practicing gratitude can reduce depression and anxiety and give you a more positive outlook on life, even if your circumstances don't change.[11]

You can practice thankfulness and gratitude with simple disciplines like:

Making a daily list of three things you are grateful for.
Paying attention to how God brought a blessing into your life today.
Writing letters (or text messages) saying thank you to people who have helped you over the years.
Singing a worship song, thanking God for His faithfulness to you.

What blessings do you have that you take for granted?

### *Turn your "if only" into an "even if"*

Several years ago, the Lord brought a godly woman, Linda, into my life who taught me a lot about contentment. I've known Linda through deep loss and hardship: family and marriage conflict, health crises, rejection, and the death of one of her children. I've seen her grieve and call out to the Lord in pain, but somehow maintain a heart of joy and contentment.

The obscure book of Habakkuk is one of Linda's favorite parts of the Bible. Why? Because God used this prophet's testimony to help Linda pivot from living with an "if only" to an "even if . . ." Linda writes: "As the book of Habakkuk progresses, this dear prophet moves from challenging God to worshiping Him. . . . The book ends with the prophet's statement of faith. He declares that even if everything is stripped away from him, all his security, everything that gives him sustenance . . . 'Yet I will exult in the Lord, I will *rejoice* in the God of my salvation'" (Hab. 3:18).[12]

Surrender means that we learn through trial and over the course of years that even if God never gives us what we think will bring happiness, He is with us, He is good, and He is enough. This is, once again, why surrender is only possible to the extent that we know Jesus, walk with Him, and learn to trust Him.

Right after he described his contented heart, Paul wrote that he could do all things by the strength of Christ. Paul's secret of contentment and Linda's secret of "even if" came through their persistent and relentless pursuit to know Jesus. Surrender of idols and intimacy with God go hand in hand.

I once heard a pastor say, "I know that Jesus is all I need, but I don't yet know Him well enough for Him to be all that I have." I heard this statement decades ago, when I was in a season of discontentment. Obviously, it stuck with me because I so often reflect on it. I cannot find contentment until I know Jesus so intimately that I can let go of the things I cling to. This has been an ongoing process in my life. Pursuing Jesus and letting go. Each season brings new things the Lord asks me to bring before Him, prompting an even deeper awareness of how much I need Jesus. As the worship song declares, "Lord, I need You. . . . Every hour I need You!"[13]

Our "if onlys" never go away on their own. If not surrendered, they morph into the next thing we believe will make us happy or sour into a life of disappointment or bitterness. By asking you to hold your desires and longings with open hands, God is not taking something away from you, but inviting you to grab onto something far greater and more lasting.

Jesus Himself showed us how to do this:

> For the joy set before him he endured the cross, scorning its shame, and sat down at the right hand of the throne of God. Consider him who endured such opposition from sinners, so that you will not grow weary and lose heart. (Heb. 12:2–3)

## Application Exercise:

---

How has marriage, sex, or singleness become a "god thing" instead of a "good thing"?

Write down your "if only":

What do you need to grieve in order to surrender your "if only"?

Write down blessings you take for granted that can help you work toward contentment.

What would it take for you to move from an "if only" to an "even if" mindset in your relationship with God?

Here are a couple of examples:

*Jarrod*:

I am continually frustrated by the lack of sex in my marriage. I am realizing that I look at sex as a need and not as a gift.

My "if only": If only my wife were more sexually responsive, I could be happy.

I need to grieve that marriage isn't what I thought it would be.

I need to grieve my belief that my sexual desires would be met through my wife.

I need to grieve that I still struggle with lust even within marriage.

I am thankful for:

The friendship and intimacy I have with my wife

The Holy Spirit who helps me in times of sadness and temptation

The sexual experiences I do have with my wife

A wife who wants to work on our marriage

Good friends who encourage me on this journey

Pursuing contentment:

I can move toward "even if my wife never changes" only as I understand what sex has come to mean to me and find God-honoring ways of addressing my longings. I need to learn to not take "not tonight" as a personal rejection from my wife.

*Alison:*

As a thirty-eight-year-old never married woman, I realize that I look at marriage and sex as if they will solve all of my problems. This has led to envy toward others and anger toward God for not giving me a spouse.

My "if only": If only God brought me a husband, I wouldn't have to be sad and lonely.

I need to grieve:

Feeling like I don't fit in

My dreams of feeling like someone chose me

Not having the life my parents wanted me to have

Not having biological children

I am thankful for:

My two best friends who make me feel like I am part of their families

My church community

My nephews, who are like children to me
The flexibility I have in my schedule that allows me to be more plugged into community and ministry
My married friends, who remind me that marriage has its own challenges!

Pursuing contentment:

I can move to an "even if" perspective with the Lord if I really, truly get an eternal perspective on things. Marriage feels so real and permanent, but it helps me to realize that this life is short. Even good marriages will one day end. I also need to learn to take the family of God more seriously. I need to foster relationships that feel like brothers and sisters, not just casual acquaintances.

## Passages to Study:

---

***Read 2 Peter 1:3–4.***

Write the passage in your own words:

Do you live like you have everything you need by God's divine power? Why or why not?

***Read Genesis 17, 22, and Hebrews 11:17–19.***

What do you think was Abraham's "if only"?

How did Abraham wrestle with his "if only"?

How did Abraham have the faith to move to the posture of "even if"?

What do you believe God is asking you to trust Him with?

## Questions for personal reflection and discussion:

1. What messages do we get from the culture encouraging us to worship sex and relationships instead of honoring them? Do you agree that the church has often Christianized these messages instead of challenging them? Why or why not?
2. Do you agree that sex is not a need? Why or why not?
3. In what ways has the Western church elevated the nuclear family above the church family? What is the fallout of this?
4. Why does the journey to contentment require both seasons of blessing and seasons of lacking?
5. Describe a difficult situation in your life in which you are learning to be content.
6. What is the role of grief and lament in your own journey toward contentment?
7. What are some practical ways that you can focus on your blessings in this season?
8. How is contentment the antidote to idolatry?

CHAPTER 7

# Surrendered Wisdom

When my children were little, we gave them bedtimes. Although they tried to delay the inevitable, Mike and I worked to stay consistent in getting them ready for bed at the same time most evenings. As my sons got older, they no longer had bedtimes; we gave them curfews. Now, as adults, they have neither.

When we are young and immature, we need guidelines (or rules) that reinforce and teach us principles. In my parenting, the rules were the bedtime and the curfew. The principle I wanted to reinforce was the wisdom of getting enough rest. As my sons grew and matured, we let go of the rules, trusting them to use wisdom in honoring the principle.

## RULES AND PRINCIPLES

Now let's apply this to sexuality. Often within the church community we focus on the rules around sexuality and fail to teach principles. In your own journey, you may have very specific questions about rules like:

How far is too far to go in a dating relationship?
Is it wrong to masturbate?

Is God okay with a married couple using sex toys?

Do I use a friend's preferred names and pronouns?

Sexual morality is very important to God, as we covered in chapter 4. But honoring God with your sexuality needs to go beyond debating and following rules. Here is why.

**1. Not everything is black and white.** If you ask ten sincere Christians the questions above, you might get ten unique responses. There are many things the Bible is very clear about, and others that rely on the application of principles, sometimes principles that appear to be conflicting. The question of masturbation might be an example of this. The Bible tells us that God created our humanity, including our sexuality. He created the increase of testosterone and other physiological changes that prompt sexual desire in adolescence. God doesn't want us to carry shame about our sexuality or our bodies. But fostering sexual thoughts and experiences outside of covenant violates God's design for sex. These two principles can seem to conflict for the single Christian flooded with sexual desire, trying to live with sexual integrity.

**2. Maturity keeps us grounded in a shifting world.** When I was a child, most people did not consider cohabitation as morally acceptable. The law did not acknowledge any relationship apart from marriage, and very few people chose to move in together instead of getting married. But times have changed. Living together is now almost expected, even if it's intended to be a step toward marriage. Even many evangelicals are following along with this trend. Paul encouraged the Ephesian Christians to become mature, like Christ, in every respect so that they wouldn't be tossed like infants, back and forth by the winds of culture (see Eph. 4:14–16). Rules change with the world, but maturity is rooted in God's unchanging love and truth, able to discern the lies of the culture in every age.

**3. Rules alone foster a posture of obedience rather than intimacy.** When we mature beyond rules, we begin to embrace God's heart. Rules tend to be fear-based. Principles communicate intention and design. For example, a woman is unhappy in her marriage. She wants to know the "rule" of when she is allowed to divorce, so she listens to a few podcasts and asks her friends if her husband's lack of sensitivity is a form of emotional abuse. This woman's mindset is on how to get out of her unhappy marriage while keeping the rules. Instead, God wants her to mature into the posture of "Lord, what is Your will for my life and marriage? I want to honor You."

## GROWING UP IN CHRIST

The writers of the New Testament letters to the early church (1 Corinthians, Colossians, and Hebrews) expressed frustration that these Christians were still immature, not growing as they should have been. They were Christians but they were baby Christians, unable or unwilling to accept the deeper truths the apostles wanted to share with them. Instead, they were arguing over rules and dividing over differences.

In the sphere of Christian sexuality, I sometimes see the same dynamic. We seem content to argue over the rules of biblical sexuality rather than pressing into the deeper surrender of what it means to glorify God in everything that we do. You can keep all of the "rules" about biblical sexuality and still have a heart that is far from God's intentions in this area of your life. Honoring God with your sexuality begins with obeying the rules but must mature far beyond. I would argue that the Christian married couple who hasn't cheated on each other and refuses to consider divorce but lacks

*You can keep all of the "rules" about biblical sexuality and still have a heart that is far from God's intentions in this area of your life.*

the love of Christ toward each other falls far short of God's design for their marriage. In a similar way, the single Christian who avoids porn and sex but is isolated and bitter is not walking in the fullness God designed for her.

In this chapter, I want to lay out a vision for what it looks like to grow into a Christian who has matured past the rules. Please note, this doesn't mean that the rules don't apply. My grown sons no longer need a bedtime, but they are still bound by the unchanging truth that their bodies require rest. In the same way, maturing beyond the rules doesn't negate the biblical boundaries God has given us for our sexuality, but calls us to a deeper application of them. Let me give you an example from my own life.

As I shared, I grew up in a Christian home where my parents had many rules for our family about what we could watch on TV. This was back in the day when there was no streaming or recording; we chose what to watch from the weekly booklet *TV Guide*. My parents went through the weekly guide and circled shows we were allowed to watch. No soap operas, no shows with violence, and no game shows (I still don't know why we couldn't watch those). As I got older, I loved the freedom of watching whatever I wanted. In college and graduate school, I was hooked on all the shows my friends watched, including now-classics like *Seinfeld* and *Friends*. I noticed themes that I knew were not honoring God, but I reasoned that I was old enough to weed those out in my thinking. I had freedom in Christ.

***God wants you to become a man or woman of wisdom, discernment, and grace.***

A decade later, as I became a parent and began to mature in my walk with the Lord, I could no longer watch the same shows I once enjoyed. This time, it wasn't because my parents might find out or out of fear of punishment, but because of love. As I grew in my relationship with Jesus, my appetites changed. I became grieved at the references to things like casual sex and pornography. I still have the same freedom in Christ that I did as a young adult, but I now have the maturity to use that freedom in a way that honors God.

This, my friend, is where God wants to take His children. In your own life, God desires for you to mature beyond just keeping the rules about sexuality. He wants you to surrender to such an extent that your posture and purpose is set on honoring Him and bringing Him glory in everything you do. He wants you to become a man or woman of wisdom, discernment, and grace. I hope that through the journey of this book, you are beginning to see God's heart for sexuality—the greater principle and purpose behind the rules of biblical sexuality.

## HOW DO WE BECOME MATURE?

### *Humble yourself*

The first step to seeking maturity is to realize how far we are from it. The English word for "sophomore" is the strange combination of two Latin words: wise fool. Sophomores are second year students who learned enough in their first year to think they know something but are not yet experienced enough to realize how much they don't know.

Christians run the risk of being lifelong sophomores in our faith. Knowing the rules can limit our awareness of how little we actually know of God's heart and how to honor Him.

I love how Solomon says it: "The beginning of wisdom is this: Get wisdom" (Prov. 4:7). In other words, you will never get wisdom if you don't have the humility to realize you need it.

This humility is not just a onetime step but must be an ongoing posture of our hearts. Solomon's life is perhaps the greatest warning to us to never become secure in wisdom. It's a choice every day to be hungry for God's guidance instead of trusting our own understanding and thoughts.

### *The constant use of God's Word*

"Anyone who lives on milk, being still an infant, is not acquainted with the teaching about righteousness. But solid food is for the mature, who by constant use have trained themselves to distinguish good from evil" (Heb. 5:13–14). Babies need predigested food, a.k.a. milk. Only adults can chew and digest their own food. The writer of Hebrews uses this metaphor to challenge us as Christians to become mature.

When you listen to a sermon or read a book, you are consuming pre-digested spiritual food. It's fed to you from someone else. That's not bad and is where we all begin with our spiritual appetite, but maturity means that we read, grapple with, and learn to apply God's Word to our own lives.

Don't get me wrong. I love learning from other people and believe it's an important part of our Christian life. But when we learn from other people, we don't just swallow what they said—we go back to God's Word to see these truths ourselves (as the Bereans did in Acts 17). By this exercise, we become mature, able to discern good and evil, even within gray areas.

A few years ago, popular author and pastor Francis Chan made a jarring statement in a message. "People, I'm not your Moses." He was addressing Christians who constantly asked him, "You've been with Jesus. What did He say?" Instead, Chan challenged, "Why haven't you been with Him?"

We have access to so many teachers, books, sermons, and podcasts that many of us have never developed the muscle of seeking the Lord, studying Scripture, and applying it to our own lives. You cannot become mature if you are living on secondhand knowledge of God.

### *Learn from life experiences*

One of my mentors said to me, "Juli, you've made a lot of mistakes. But I've never seen you make the same one twice." Maturity comes from the insistence to always "fail forward." I'm convinced that no experience of pain or sin will ever be wasted if we surrender it to God. Maturity comes through reflecting on life—the good and the bad.

This doesn't mean you have to be old to be mature. I met one young man who has made it a practice to ask every older person he meets questions like, "If you could tell yourself one thing when you were my age, what would it be?" and "What is one regret you have in your life?" Read biographies, seek mentors, and learn from what you see playing out in the lives you witness.

### *Respond to God's leading*

"The LORD confides in those who fear him" (Ps. 25:14). I love this verse. I want to be someone God can confide in, sharing His plans and revealing His ways. Jesus said in John 14, "Those who accept my commandments and obey them are the ones who love me. And because they love me, my Father will love them. And I will love them and reveal myself to each of them" (v. 21 NLT).

If we want God to give us discernment to hear His voice, we need to begin with obeying what we already know. The Bible says that we can suppress the voice of the Holy Spirit by not yielding to Him.

Maybe you wonder how you can love your spouse sexually when you are not attracted to her anymore. You want God's wisdom and healing, but you are looking at pornography. Don't expect God to give you wisdom about your marriage and sex life if you continue to ignore what He already has clearly revealed.

## APPLYING WISDOM TO QUESTIONS CHRISTIANS OFTEN ASK

Let's take all of this and apply it to some of the issues Christians often ask about.

### *How far is too far in dating?*

Ten years ago, when someone asked me this question, I referred back to what I learned growing up and how I tried to manage this boundary in my dating relationships. The "rule" was you shouldn't touch each other anywhere a modest bathing suit would cover. I've not only changed my mind but now look back on my dating experiences with regret. I was navigating my relationships based on a Christian version of cultural wisdom rather than biblical principles.

Paul wrote in 1 Thessalonians 4:3–6a, "It is God's will that you should be sanctified: that you should avoid sexual immorality; that each of you should learn to control your own body in a way that is holy and honorable, not in passionate lust like the pagans, who do not know God; and that in this matter no one should wrong or take advantage of a brother or sister."

God's will for you is not just that you avoid having sex with someone, but that you control your body in a way that is holy and honorable and that you never take advantage of a brother or sister in Christ. Their body does not belong to you, but belongs to God. Instead of trying to hold the line on not going too far physically, think about the person you are dating first and foremost as a brother or sister in the Lord—as building a good friendship that might lead to marriage.

If we are honest, we would admit that most physical affection in dating relationships is about self-exploration and satisfaction. It's not honoring the other person or God. Remember that sexual activity is not primarily a way of personal satisfaction or even of expressing affection. It is a sign of covenant. If you want a clear answer on "how far is too far," wisdom would tell you not to do anything that prepares your body for sex. Another way to state it is: Don't do anything in private that would not be appropriate to do in public. You don't need a "running start" for your honeymoon. If you end up getting married, there will be a journey of learning to love each other sexually. I've yet to meet a couple who said how glad they were that they experimented with each other sexually while dating but have met many married Christians who regret pushing the boundaries.

Most Christian couples struggle not just with physical boundaries, but also with emotional and spiritual boundaries. Some couples view dating as a way to try on marriage. They may not live together, but they treat each other as if they are "half married." They share deep secrets, become threatened if there is any distance in the relationship, have pet names for each other, and celebrate anniversaries. Some Christian women see their boyfriend as their "spiritual leader"—almost as a quasi-husband.

*If you want a clear answer on "how far is too far," don't do anything in private that would not be appropriate to do in public.*

Dating is not "marriage light." On Instagram, author Debra Fileta clarifies, "The dating stage isn't about intimacy—it's about investigation."[1] As you consider your dating relationships, don't just think about the physical boundaries, but also the emotional boundaries and expectations that put your heart (and the person you are dating) at a greater risk for heartache and regret.

### *Does my spouse owe me sex?*

Many people point to this passage in 1 Corinthians 7 to make the case that having sex is an obligation in marriage:

> The husband should fulfill his marital duty to his wife, and likewise the wife to her husband. The wife does not have authority over her own body but yields it to her husband. In the same way, the husband does not have authority over his own body but yields it to his wife. Do not deprive each other except perhaps by mutual consent and for a time, so that you may devote yourselves to prayer. Then come together again so that Satan will not tempt you because of your lack of self-control. (vv. 3–5)

When this passage becomes a rule instead of a principle, it leads to entitlement and duty sex, both of which undermine the more important principle that marriage is meant to be a reflection of God's covenant love. God's desire for a married couple is for them to grow in intimacy.

I love how The Message[2] paraphrases Paul's teaching in the same passage:

> The marriage bed must be a place of mutuality—the husband seeking to satisfy his wife, the wife seeking to satisfy her husband. Marriage is not a place to "stand up for your rights." Marriage is a decision to serve the other, whether in bed or out.

The greater biblical principle is this: Sexual intimacy is an important part of marriage, and both the husband and wife should invest in it. Instead of duty sex or entitlement, it is the call to pursue oneness sexually.

Married sex doesn't always meet all of your needs. Most marriages struggle with mismatched sexual desires, difficulty communicating about sex, physical problems like painful sex, sexual temptations, and difficulty experiencing orgasm. Still others navigate complexities in the wake of sexual trauma, sexual addictions, or significant medical complications.

***When sex is "good," it allows a couple to delight in each other. But when sex is difficult, it invites couples to experience the goodness of unconditional love.***

Without exception, every passage about Christian marriage and Christian love teaches both husband and wife to be unselfish, kind, and humble, looking not only to their own interests, but also to the interests of others (Phil. 2:4). This is to be a mutual unselfishness that applies to all areas of a Christian marriage.

If your spouse was exactly like you and

wanted sex whenever you did and how you did, you could have a great sex life without ever needing to learn how to be unselfish. But the natural differences between you and your spouse, compounded by the brokenness in our world, means that you can't work on your sex life without learning to love sacrificially. This kind of unselfish love in your sex life might include:

Postponing sex because your spouse isn't ready.
Working on your sexual relationship even when it is difficult.
Practicing the self-control to learn to arouse your spouse sexually and not only focus on your own needs.
Being patient with your spouse's healing journey.
Persevering through seasons in which your spouse is unable to engage sexually because of emotional or physical challenges.

When sex is "good," it allows a couple to delight in each other. But when sex is difficult, it invites couples to experience the goodness of unconditional love. Our Creator crafted humans with the capacity to love as He loves—sacrificially. His desire is for us to imitate Him and learn to love that way.

I have found it helpful to differentiate between the importance of sexual activity in marriage versus working on sexual intimacy. Sexual activity focuses on what is happening in your body. Are we having enough sex? Are we sexually compatible? Am I sexually attracted to my spouse? Sexual intimacy focuses on the journey of becoming more vulnerable and developing a shared experience through both the trials and joys of sex. There are some situations in which engaging in sexual activity will sabotage intimacy. For example, if sex is physically painful or if it triggers traumatic memories, the worst thing you can do is just go through the motions. You are training your brain to associate your marriage bed with fear and pain. Instead, focus on what it looks like to build safety and intimacy.

Sometimes our greatest sexual intimacy can be cultivated when sexual activity isn't going so well. Challenges like infertility, feeling rejected by your spouse, or battling memories from the past can cause us to stop having sex for a while so that we can actually communicate about the journey of what it means to be "naked and unashamed" with each other.

***Are sex toys okay in a Christian marriage?***

Living out the covenant of marriage can involve hard work. God has given a husband and wife the journey and experience of sexual intimacy as a gift for them to enjoy on the journey. The dopamine, adrenaline, and oxytocin our brains release during sexual arousal and climax help a husband and wife bond as they weather the challenges of marriage. Sex is supposed to be fun, beautiful, exciting, and pleasurable.

God's desire is for a married couple to experience great pleasure! Just consider the erotic poetry in the Song of Songs. In one passage (4:16–5:1), the husband and wife have just enjoyed sexual pleasure together. The bride says:

> Awake, north wind,
>     and come, south wind!
> Blow on my garden,
>     that its fragrance may spread everywhere.
> Let my beloved come into his garden
>     and taste its choice fruits.

The groom responds:

> I have come into my garden, my sister, my bride;
>     I have gathered my myrrh with my spice.
> I have eaten my honeycomb and my honey;
>     I have drunk my wine and my milk.

And then God speaks over them:

> Eat, friends, and drink;
> drink your fill of love.

God made the marriage relationship a safe place for a husband and wife to explore, experiment, laugh, and get lost in sensational sex. There is nothing spiritual or moral about limiting sexual pleasure in marriage. God is the greatest proponent of your pleasure—not the pleasure that is sweet for a season, but the deep, profound satisfaction that only grows sweeter with time.

As you've learned throughout this book, God calls for the pleasure and celebration of sex to only be between a husband and wife within marriage. This includes not just in the flesh, but also what we think about and look at.

But what about sex toys? The Bible is silent on this topic, so we have to apply biblical principles. The most helpful biblical principle for me with this question is Paul's teaching in 1 Corinthians 10:23–24:

> "I have the right to do anything," you say—but not everything is beneficial. "I have the right to do anything"—but not everything is constructive. No one should seek their own good, but the good of others.

There are many things in marriage that you are free to enjoy together. When you are not sure whether something is okay, put it through Paul's filter:

Is this beneficial? Is it good for me? For my spouse? Is it good for our marriage?

Is it constructive? Does it build our marriage? Is it loving?

Are sex toys good for your marriage? Do they build intimacy or get in the way of it? I've seen situations when both have been true.

I know one woman who has great difficulty experiencing climax in her marriage. She tried using a vibrator, which helped her with this situation. Both the husband and wife agree that using this "toy" builds intimacy in their marriage and helps them experience great pleasure together.

In another situation, the husband and wife have come to rely on always using sex toys. Both have a history of heavy pornography use, and they have never learned to enjoy the gift of each other's bodies. The focus is all on the physical experience of sex rather than on the journey of intimacy. For them, sex toys are hindering sexual intimacy rather than encouraging it.

*If you and your spouse disagree on a "gray area," you will have to listen and learn to love each other through the decision.*

This means that for some couples, a sexual act will be fine, and for another couple, the same act isn't right for them. Ultimately, a couple needs to seek God's wisdom for their own marriage. If you and your spouse disagree on a "gray area," you will have to listen and learn to love each other through the decision.

***Is masturbation wrong?***

Everywhere I speak, people ask me this question. It is the subject of our most downloaded podcast and accessed blog post. Obviously, people are curious about masturbation.

The topic of masturbation is often covered in a cloud of shame—shame for past behavior, shame for having sexual desire, and shameful memories of getting caught in the act. Interestingly, God never addresses masturbation in the Bible, and we would assume people wondered about it back then. While people often want a blanket yes or no answer to the question of masturbation, we need take on the deeper issues of what it means to honor God with our sexuality.

God's design for sex matters. As you have been learning, sex is the bodily symbol of two lives covenanted together as a metaphor of Christ's covenant with the church (see Eph. 5:31–32). Any genital sexual expression that is not a celebration of covenant falls short of why God created sex. But when we understand the connection of sex to covenant, we realize that masturbation is, at best, an incomplete expression of sexuality.

Your thoughts matter. For most people, masturbation is paired with sexual thoughts, fantasies, or pornography. Jesus is extremely clear in Matthew 5:28: "Anyone who looks at a woman lustfully has already committed adultery with her in his heart." If masturbation involves any form of thoughts or images of someone (even imaginary) you are not in covenant with, you are nurturing lust in your heart.

Your conscience and convictions matter. In his letters to both the Romans and Corinthians, Paul emphasized the importance of conscience. If you are convicted by the Holy Spirit about the issue of masturbation, you need to pay attention to that conviction. On some issues of Christian living, people have different convictions. Masturbation that does not involve lustful thoughts, images, or fantasies may be one of these issues of personal conviction and can be thought of as an acceptable way of managing overwhelming temptation. Even so, remember that masturbation is not a long-term solution to sexual desire and loneliness.

Seek maturity. Think of masturbation not only as a matter of morality, but also as a matter of maturity. Your relationship with God should result in a growing sense of surrender to the work and power of the Holy Spirit in every area of your life. The goal is for you to mature in your understanding of God's design for sex, in your self-control through the Holy Spirit, and in understanding and addressing your struggles and wounds. As you do so, the urge to masturbate should become less because you are learning to control your thoughts and your body, and you are learning healthier ways to cope with loneliness and painful emotions that are often triggers.[3]

***What does it look like to be a godly man or woman?***

God could have created us with one gender. He could have created us with twenty genders. He chose instead to create male and female—two unique expressions that together share the image of God. Because God cares about male and female, so should we.

Gender has been an interesting topic for me personally. Growing up, I was a tomboy. I loved all sports and slept with a Cleveland Browns Nerf football instead of a doll. I didn't like dresses or frills or anything pink.

As I got older, I discovered other ways that I didn't fit female cultural stereotypes. I'm quiet, logical, and competitive. Others noticed that I didn't quite fit the mold. I remember giving a speech at my high school graduation. The headmaster said to my parents, "It's too bad Juli isn't a boy. She would have made a great pastor!" (My wise mother was ready with a quick reply: "Yeah, you're right. God sure made a mistake.") Once I got married, I struggled to know how I, as a type-A driven person, was supposed to be submissive to my laid-back husband. As a young bride, I attended a Bible study on how to be a godly wife. The book we were studying emphasized the domestic arts, and I remember feeling like I could never be who it seemed that God created me to be. I could write books but couldn't decorate or cook very well. I lacked skills like homemaking that seemed necessary to being a godly woman.

There is a lot of discussion among Christians about gender, not only within the transgender conversation but also as male and female relate to things like roles in marriage and ministry. You may have strong thoughts and personal convictions about this topic, as many Christians do. For the purpose of this book, I'm not going to weigh in on much of the controversy of these secondary issues. In this next section, I'll share some basic biblical principles that can inform how we steward our gender with God's glory in mind.

## THINKING THROUGH GENDER ISSUES

### *Our bodies matter*

I recently interviewed three different experts on gender and asked them each the question, "What do you think it means to be male or female?" All three of them began by referring to the body.

Postmodern thought causes us to consider the physical world as less important than our emotional and psychological experience. We are encouraged to create an internal reality that is untethered from physical reality. But God created us as souls who also have bodies. Scientists now know that every one of our cells is impacted by its sex: "The sex chromosomes are not just expressed in gonadal tissue, but are present in every cell in the body, leading to the implication that all cells have a sex!"[4] The Creator formed our bodies intentionally as part of what it means to be male and female, made in His image. We can manipulate gender with our clothing, pronouns, or even surgery, but our maleness and femaleness are stamped all over and within our bodies. We cannot understand gender without embracing the importance of our bodies, as God created male and female.

> ***God never uses the word "roles" to describe men and women. A role is like a part you learn to play. It's something you act out, not something that you become.***

### *Our gender is more than our bodies*

There is something deeply unsatisfying for me to think of myself as a woman only because I have a womb and ovaries. I want to know how to honor God as a woman in my thoughts, pursuits, and relationships. What is God uniquely expressing about Himself when male and female interact in healthy ways?

It has helped me a lot over the years to realize that God never uses the word "roles" to describe men and women. A role is like a part you learn to play. It's something you act out, not something that you become. What we do or don't do to honor God in our gender is often deeply influenced by culture, circumstances, and even our Christian subcultures. For example, I remember a podcast conversation I had with well-respected teacher Jackie Hill Perry. She explained the tension she felt as a Black woman trying to live up to a definition of godly womanhood that has been shaped by White culture.

> When I came to faith, I was interested in biblical womanhood because I came out of a world where I struggled with my gender identity. So I think it's important for me to have a theology of what it means to be a woman. It wasn't until about three or four years ago I started to see that the biblical womanhood I was introduced to was more of a White womanhood that didn't really describe me. It made me feel as if how God made me was not actually godly. I don't want to make cookies for my husband all the time, I'm not going to stay at home, I'm not going to homeschool, I don't even breastfeed. People that do that—awesome—but I drunk up this messaging that made me feel like if I don't do these things, I'm not a biblical woman.[5]

Growing in wisdom and maturity means that we become more of who *God* created us to be as male and female, not that we feel pressured by cultural stereotypes. God is ultimately interested in the posture and spirit of our hearts. Out of a surrendered heart, we will behave in ways that reflect the beauty of godly manhood and womanhood.

I think of the godly women I know who distinctly honor God in their femininity but seem to have little other traits or interests in common just by being a woman. One is an opinionated and outgoing mother of three. Another is a reserved, discerning business manager.

The same is true for godly men. A godly, masculine man can be an artsy stay-at-home dad or a shrewd businessman, committed to God's kingdom work. What they do matters far less than the heart, the spirit, and the motivation behind the details of their lives.

As a woman, what is the posture of your heart? Do you relationally draw out the best of those around you or do you try to compete with them?

As a man, are you willing to move into the world with the strength and confidence that comes from knowing and remembering God's faithfulness? Or do your insecurities keep you hiding behind passivity and bravado?

While there is variety among men and women, there is also something distinctly unique. The interplay between male and female is important in all of our relationships, but it is particularly noteworthy in marriage. The Bible is super clear that the dynamic of husband and wife, when stewarded in love, reflects the covenant relationship between Christ and His bride. These are not "roles" (e.g., the husband must be the breadwinner, the wife must bake the bread) but postures of the heart. God calls the husband to step into the responsibility and initiative of leadership and the woman into the powerful place of harnessing her influence to support and receive her husband. Both the husband and wife have to face their own unique challenges and fears to interact based on God's direction—the man facing his fear of failure and the woman facing her fear of not being in control.

(For a more comprehensive look at how this plays out in a healthy marriage, see my book *Finding the Hero in Your Husband, Revisited: Embracing Your Power in Marriage.*[6])

### *Remember that the goal is to honor God*

There is a lot to unpack regarding what it actually looks like to honor God with our gender. In recent years, a slew of writers and influencers have devoted their time to addressing issues like toxic masculinity, blurred gender expressions, and godly womanhood.[7]

Your goal should not be to express yourself in your gender, but to honor God as His creation. Ask the Lord to show you what that looks like to honor Him as a man or woman in your specific life situation and culture.

I can't stress enough the importance of asking the Lord to help you think wisely and deeply about the topics of sexuality and gender. You literally receive thousands of messages a year on what it looks like to think about these questions from a secular perspective.

## DETERMINED TO FOLLOW CHRIST

As you have been learning, surrendering your sexuality to God goes way beyond following a list of rules. It involves inviting God to reform, remake, and redeem decades of indoctrination from the culture. Discipleship is not reading a book, but the determination to follow Jesus in everything. It's a journey that takes time and commitment. It's a journey that I am still on!

In my job I'm in the position of regularly working through some of the more difficult tensions for Christians in today's sexual landscape. Please know . . . I am on the journey with you! I am still learning and still seeking God. As I seek God's wisdom personally on difficult questions, here are the four steps I often take.

**1. I ask, "What has God said?"** I search the Bible for clear teaching on the particular topic. If God is clear, then I can stop there. For example, God is clear that marriage is between a man and a woman.

**2. I ask, "What principles apply?"** While not all questions have a clear biblical answer, biblical principles weigh into every situation. The Bible does not address clearly if it's okay to attend a gay wedding. Instead, we need to search for and apply principles.

**3. I seek wisdom.** I read and listen to thought leaders and teachers. I study related research. When I'm able, I ask for personal counsel from people I trust.

**4. I follow my convictions.** I ask God to show me what His will is. Sometimes I have a clear conviction about something. Remember that a conviction from God will never violate what He has clearly revealed in His Word. God is not going to tell you to cheat on your wife or have sex with your boyfriend. Within the framework of what He has revealed in Scripture, the Holy Spirit will guide and convict us uniquely. The Bible teaches that we are to follow the convictions God gives us and also leave room for Him to convict other believers differently (see Rom. 14:21–23; Phil. 3:15).

I'm sure there is some area in your own life where you are seeking God's wisdom. God's greatest desire for you is not just to figure out the answer but to develop intimacy with Him in the process of seeking. Yes, it's easier just to have someone tell you what to do in your current situation. Developing maturity and learning to discern God's voice takes time and can feel like a struggle. But in the process, you are not only getting direction, but developing a relationship with the Lord who is truly becoming your Shepherd, leading you, guiding you, and comforting you.

### Application Exercise:

---

What is one question that represents a "gray" area of Christian sexuality that you struggle with?

Step 1: What has God said?

Are there specific Bible passages that directly apply to this question?

Step 2: What principles apply?

List biblical principles that weigh into the issue you are seeking wisdom on.

Step 3: Seek wisdom.

As you seek wisdom, make sure the person or resource is coming from a perspective of honoring God's truth.[8] As the Bible says, fearing the Lord is the very beginning of wisdom. Is there someone you personally know who can give you wisdom? What do you learn from their perspective?

Step 4: Follow your convictions.

How is the Holy Spirit personally convicting you as you seek Him on this topic?

How will you respond if other Christians are convicted differently than you are?

## Passages to Study:

---

***Read Ephesians 4:11–16.***

What does Paul say will happen to Christians who are not mature in Christ?

How have you seen this happen in your own life?

How does Paul describe Christian maturity in this passage?

How are fellow believers meant to impact each other's maturity, according to this passage?

***Read 1 Corinthians 3:1–3 and 18–23.***

What is Paul concerned about with the Corinthian church?

How does he describe the difference between worldly and godly wisdom?

How does worldy wisdom interfere with your pursuit of godly wisdom on sexuality-related issues?

## Questions for personal reflection and discussion:

---

1. What is the impact of only teaching rules on Christian sexuality without encouraging maturity?
2. Please share an example from your own spiritual walk where you've learned the rules but not been encouraged to seek maturity.
3. In what ways is the Lord calling you to grow in Christian maturity related to sexual issues?
4. Which of the examples of gray areas in this chapter most resonated with you? Why?
5. How have you settled for "predigested" spiritual truth rather than learning to seek wisdom and discernment personally?
6. How does seeking wisdom on sexual issues encourage you to *know* Jesus more personally?

CHAPTER 8

# Surrendered to Love

A few years ago, Mike and I crossed the finish line of active parenting. Our sons are all in the process of launching into adulthood. As I watch these three boys flourish as young men, I am so grateful for God's grace that has been with me throughout parenting. But as with most parents, I also have some regrets about things I wish I had handled differently. Ironically, some of those regrets centered around sexuality.

As is the case with many kids growing up in this culture, my sons have at times struggled with technology and relationships. Sometimes, I responded to these struggles with my own fear and shame rather than leading with love. My deepest regrets, which I have since shared with my adult sons, is when I made parenting about me instead of reflecting the love of Jesus.

So many times in marriage, parenting, and ministry, God has needed to teach me to lay down my agendas so that I could love well. When I look back, my greatest victories have been when I've yielded to love and my greatest regrets have been when I didn't.

## THE PRIORITY OF LOVE

Francis Schaeffer wrote, "Biblical orthodoxy without compassion is surely the ugliest thing in the world."

When it all boils down to it, the true Christian life is a life of love—love known and exchanged between us and God, and love overflowing to those around us. But how many people, looking in from the outside, would characterize Christians as people of love?

I've seen and experienced a lot of hard things over the course of decades in Christian ministry. I do not say this lightly. Nothing has grieved me more deeply than our lack of love . . . including my own.

> If I speak in the tongues of men or of angels, but do not have love, I am only a resounding gong or a clanging cymbal. If I have the gift of prophecy and can fathom all mysteries and all knowledge, and if I have a faith that can move mountains, but do not have love, I am nothing. If I give all I possess to the poor and give over my body to hardship that I may boast, but do not have love, I gain nothing. (1 Cor. 13:1–3)

When I read the Bible, I see that God's greatest call on our life is not having the right theology, standing for the right causes, doing the most good deeds, or even living the purest life. God's crowning work in our lives is that He makes us into people of love.

Surrender's last and final achievement in our lives is that we no longer wake up fighting for what we believe or what we desire, but that we say, "Lord, Your will be done." Jesus' own disciples needed this transformation. Think of His inner circle, Peter, James, and John, who right before His crucifixion were self-centered, wanting to accomplish "godly work" through ambition and hatred. Peter cut off an ear and the "sons of thunder" jockeyed to become the greatest in the kingdom of heaven.

Surrender ultimately frees us to love. We let go of our demands, our agendas, and fears and trust God who is all to do all.

As we wrap up our journey together, let's consider how our surrendered sexuality will fall short if we do not ultimately become people of love. In many ways, issues of sexuality present a great challenge to how we love within our closest relationships, when we have been hurt, and among the family of God.

## "LOVE YOUR NEIGHBOR AS YOURSELF"

Jesus told us to love our neighbor, calling us to be thoughtful, kind, and caring people. "Your neighbor" essentially includes all the people with whom you have contact—your actual neighbors, the people who live in your town, your family members, your coworkers.

When Jesus was asked more about what it means to love your neighbor, He responded by telling a story that has come to be known as the parable of the good Samaritan.

The essence of the story is this: A man traveling from Jerusalem to Jericho is attacked by robbers, who strip him, beat him, and leave him half-dead. Two different religious leaders—a priest and a Levite—pass by the injured man but do not help him. Finally, a Samaritan, who is generally despised by Jews, stops and cares for the wounded man. He bandages his wounds, takes him to an inn, and pays for his care.

The people in our daily life and local proximity are hurting in ways that we likely don't even notice. Love means taking the time to look, to listen, and to care.

### *Love surrenders our agendas*

It's fascinating that Jesus chose to make the hero of this story a Samaritan, who His audience, the Jewish leaders, had no respect for. Jesus used the kindness and compassion of a fictional pagan to convict the people who claimed to follow God. Jesus didn't just tell a story about what the Samaritan did, but also pointed out two religious people who did not show love. Ironically, sometimes religious people are the worst at loving our neighbors. Here's why: To love well, we need to be willing to surrender our agendas.

***Without realizing it, we can assume an agenda against evil that keeps us from the most powerful source of God's work—His love pouring through us.***

These two religious leaders didn't stop to love because they were busy doing "God things." Let's imagine that one had to speak at an important conference. Another had a group of people waiting for him that he couldn't let down.

We often devise our own ways of solving the world's problems and they seldom have to do with loving people well. We all have "good works" we think will fix our families, our communities, and our friends. But how often do those agendas, goals, and plans get in the way of noticing and serving the people God puts in our path?

It is also very likely that the priest and Levite in Jesus' story didn't help the man on the side of the road because they were afraid of violating their religious standards. Perhaps they believed the beaten man was actually dead, and according to the Jewish law, a priest couldn't touch a dead body without becoming unclean. But as Jesus so often modeled, legalism is the enemy of love.

I've run across this many times in ministry on sexual issues. Sincere Christians feel as though they are compromising if they show kindness and care to someone who is living in sexual sin. "I'm afraid to ask my hair stylist about her wife. If I do, isn't it like I'm agreeing with her lifestyle?"

Sometimes our commitment to truth can make us feel as though we need to hesitate in showing love or kindness to someone with whom we disagree—even our own children. When Jesus tells us to love our neighbors as we love ourselves, He is asking us to lay down our sense of moral self-righteousness. Without realizing it, we can assume an agenda against evil that keeps us from the most powerful source of God's work—His love pouring through us.

One friend shared the truth of this in her own life:

> My sister and I were very close. Then, over the course of two weeks, she separated from her husband, came out as bisexual, and renounced her faith. I argued and pleaded with her throughout this time, and she began to hate and resent me, cutting me out of her life completely. Based on the advice of a trusted counselor, I decided to make it my goal not to argue with her, but to show her gentle kindness and respect and to pray for her. For five long years she spiraled into addiction and erratic sexual behavior. But then one day she suddenly asked me to dinner and told me she'd joined a recovery group. She asked for my forgiveness and told me that I had shown her more love than anyone she had ever known. While I'm still praying for her salvation, I'm so grateful that her life is now more stable and safe, and that we have a loving relationship once again.

It is not our job to judge or to convert the people around us. That is God's business. If we take on that agenda, we will feel conflicted about showing honor and kindness to someone who doesn't know God. It is actually only through kindness, combined with a life of personal integrity, that people will see God working in our lives.

One young woman who grew up in a Christian home shares how her church reacted when she confessed a struggle with sexual sin.

> My church put on this face of "We love everybody and we are all about grace." That was always the message. But when I started confessing to people in the church, "I'm dealing with this right now, it's really hard for me, I don't know what to do," the only thing that they could seem to think about was how to convert me back to their way of thinking: "Well, you're wrong, because we already know the answer." Nobody

> was like, "Okay, let's just talk this through. It's your life, and whatever you decide we will still care about you." The only thing they cared about in the conversation was giving me "the answer" and making sure they got me back on "the right path." Treating the whole thing like a debate instead of a conversation.[1]

Do you have an agenda on how you need to "fix" a family member, confront society's evils, or uphold God's standard for sexuality? Could it be that your agenda (even if it seems to be a righteous one) distracts you from obeying Jesus' most basic commandment of love?

***Love your enemy***

Jesus looks at the highest expression of love not in how we love our neighbors, but how we love our enemies.

> "You have heard that it was said, 'Love your neighbor and hate your enemy.' But I tell you, love your enemies and pray for those who persecute you, that you may be children of your Father in heaven. He causes his sun to rise on the evil and the good, and sends rain on the righteous and the unrighteous. If you love those who love you, what reward will you get? Are not even the tax collectors doing that? And if you greet only your own people, what are you doing more than others? Do not even pagans do that? Be perfect, therefore, as your heavenly Father is perfect." (Matt. 5:43–48)

What a high standard, particularly when we've been wounded or betrayed!

Our greatest pain and rejection often comes from someone we trusted or once deeply loved. A spouse who cheated. A friend who slandered. A leader who deceived. A parent who abused. For many of us, our deepest wounds have come not from a world that we expect to oppose us, but from those we expected to treat us with care and kindness.

What does it practically look like to love someone who has become an enemy? In this situation, Jesus calls us to a very unique kind of love that He also perfectly displayed for us when He was betrayed, denied, persecuted, and hated.

***Jesus told us to always forgive. But forgiveness does not mean going back into a situation that would continue to be harmful.***

Don't take revenge

The most natural thing to do is to treat people the way we think they should be treated.

> If you cheat on me, don't expect me to be faithful to you.
>
> If you slandered me, then I'll do the same to you.

Being God's children means that we don't play by these rules. There is a time to be angry and to confront evil, but loving your enemy means that you don't take it upon yourself to punish or curse your enemy.

Remember this very important caveat: Loving your enemies does not mean the absence of boundaries or justice. If someone is hurting you emotionally, physically, or sexually, loving them does not mean staying silent or remaining in a harmful situation.

God has put spiritual and civic systems in place in order to address evil and injustice. Even if our Christian leaders and civic authorities are imperfect, their job is to intervene to confront violence and to protect people from those who engage in evil.

Jesus told us to always forgive. This means that we don't harbor bitterness in our hearts toward our enemy. Instead of taking revenge, we leave judgment and revenge to God. But forgiveness does not mean going back into a situation that would continue to be harmful.

We also see this example in Jesus' life. While He showed love and compassion to people, He did not entrust Himself to them because He knew what was in their hearts (John 2:24).

Forgiveness and reconciliation are not the same thing. There are certainly times when a relationship can be restored after infidelity, betrayal, or other harmful behavior, but that process requires a genuine change of heart. Only when there has been true repentance and the willingness to slowly build trust can you be reconciled with someone who has hurt you. Loving your enemy may mean loving from a distance—physically and emotionally. Even if you are working toward reconciliation, boundaries are an important element of rebuilding trust.

Love does not mean rushing through the process of forgiveness or reconciliation. A husband who just found out about his wife's infidelity is not ready to forgive and certainly can't yet move toward reconciliation. We can't forgive until we've come to terms with the harm that has been done. And it may take many months to discern whether or not his wife is repentant or just sorry that she got caught.

### Pray for your enemies

One thing we can do from a distance is pray for and bless our enemies. Praying for our enemies accomplishes three things:

1. Prayer softens our hearts. It's difficult to pray for someone and stay angry.

2. Prayer impacts the spiritual landscape of the situation. I don't understand why, but God has ordered the universe in such a way that our prayers move His heart. Through prayer, strongholds are broken, lives are changed, and revival can be ushered in.

3. Prayer surrenders the situation to God. Prayer reminds us that not only can God change our circumstances, but He is also the Judge

> between us. Only through the prayer of surrendering the situation to God can I have a heart that doesn't hold on to bitterness or seek revenge.

Even as we are called to bless our enemies, we are also told to leave room for God to repay them for the evil they have done (Rom. 12:19). Sexual abuse is a great evil. How do you bless someone who stole your innocence or betrayed your trust? Ultimately, we cannot love our enemies unless we release our desire for revenge, trusting that it is God who is going to make things right.

Rachael Denhollander has become a powerful voice for victims of sexual abuse. She was the first among gymnasts to accuse Dr. Larry Nassar, which eventually led to his conviction and sentence. Before Nassar was sentenced, Rachael delivered a 36-minute, heart-wrenching victim's statement to Nassar that included this:

> You spoke of praying for forgiveness. But Larry, if you have read the Bible you carry, you know forgiveness does not come from doing good things, as if good deeds can erase what you have done. It comes from repentance, which requires facing and acknowledging the truth about what you have done in all of its utter depravity and horror without mitigation, without excuse, without acting as if good deeds can erase what you have seen in this courtroom today.
>
> The Bible you speak carries a final judgment where all of God's wrath and eternal terror is poured out on men like you. Should you ever reach the point of truly facing what you have done, the guilt will be crushing. And that is what makes the gospel of Christ so sweet. Because it extends grace and hope and mercy where none should be found. And it will be there for you.
>
> I pray you experience the soul-crushing weight of guilt so you may

someday experience true repentance and true forgiveness from God, which you need far more than forgiveness from me—though I extend that to you as well.[2]

If you have been deeply harmed by someone, God understands that your immediate desire and prayer might be for them to suffer miserably (this is essentially what David prayed for his enemies in many of the psalms). But in time, God will ask you to surrender not only your desire for revenge, but your anger. Anger is a necessary stop on the journey of healing. But by its very definition, righteous anger will always have a shelf life. If we hold on to it, it sours into bitterness and contempt.

By the supernatural work of God, I know people who over time have moved from anger to compassion for the people who have most harmed them.

***Love for the family of God***

On the night Jesus was betrayed, He had a final, intimate meal with His disciples. The apostle John recorded many of His final words to them in John 13–17. Jesus' overarching theme to His followers was love—to abide in the love of the Father and to love one another as He has loved them. During this time, Jesus prayed for them, and He prayed for us! It's the only words of Jesus that specifically mention "those who *will* believe in me." Guess what He prayed for? "That all of them may be one" (John 17:21).

Jesus doesn't just call us to love our Christian brothers and sisters but to be in unity with them. How do we describe unity? It is "the quality or state of not being multiple: oneness."[3]

Please notice that we are not called to be unified with the world. Paul makes this clear in 2 Corinthians 6:14: "Do not be yoked together with unbelievers. For what do righteousness and wickedness have in common? Or what fellowship can light have with darkness?"

Unity is a totally different level of love. It still includes kindness and serving each other, but adds to it the ongoing effort of seeking peace with one another.

Paul writes to the Ephesians, "Make every effort to keep the unity of the Spirit through the bond of peace. There is one body and one Spirit, just as you were called to one hope when you were called; one Lord, one faith, one baptism; one God and Father of all, who is over all and through all and in all" (4:3–6).

Notice that Paul writes that we should make every effort to *keep* the unity of the Spirit, not that we should *create* this unity. Repeatedly the Bible uses the terms "family" and "body" to describe the people of God. These word pictures show us that we are already unified.

Families, no matter our disagreements, are forever tied together by the same genetics and shared history. The metaphor of a body is even more powerful. No part of your body can function if it is separated from the rest of the body. There is no independence, but every part takes its direction from the head. The same is meant to be true in the body of Christ. Christ is our head. We cannot function apart from Him and without each other. In Christ, we are inseparable.

Not everyone who attends church or even says "I am a Christian" has surrendered their life to the Lord, but debated theological issues should never divide us if we are truly committed to the lordship of Jesus Christ. Even when Paul was teaching the early Christians, they had disagreements that threatened to divide. Paul was very concerned about these Christians, writing, "If you are always biting and devouring one another, watch out! Beware of destroying one another" (Gal. 5:15 NLT).

He might issue the same warning to us. The issues we disagree over today feel heavy and significant, but we need to understand that the greater threat may be our lack of love and unity. We argue over sexual issues like biblical grounds for divorce and remarriage, pronoun use, what it means to be a biblical man or woman, whether the term "gay Christian" is acceptable, and if it's okay to attend a same-sex wedding. While these are important topics on which to seek biblical truth, it grieves my heart to see blogs, podcasts, and books tearing down other Christians over what we disagree about.

### Return to what unites us

A few years ago, I was asked to help a ministry navigate an internal conflict. This organization had been founded to reach out to women in sex trafficking and prostitution and was now struggling with some issues related to serving biological men identifying as women. Some serving within the ministry felt that they should honor a person's pronouns and presentation of their gender, while others believed strongly that this would be a compromise of their Christian calling. This ministry that had been a blessing to our city was on the verge of collapse, with people leaving who had strong convictions on both sides of the argument.

As I thought and prayed about the situation, one phrase kept going through my mind. *What unites us is far more important than what divides us.* Did it matter whether or not this ministry used preferred pronouns and served biological males who identified as females? Yes. There are valid convictions and fears on both sides. But these disagreements matter less than the call to serve the hurting and marginalized in our community.

In many situations, division is far more demonic than getting an issue wrong.

What is it that unifies us? In a word, it is Christ, the fulfillment of all of the Law and all of the Prophets. We do not unite because we call ourselves "Christians" or even because we work for the same ministry. We unite because we have been transformed by Jesus. Francis Chan explains, "We share a common miracle. We were weak and dead; then everything changed. We experience a grace that leaves us speechless."[4]

And so in our disagreements, we begin with our love and devotion for

Him. We return to His teaching, ask for His help, model His example of love, grace, and forgiveness toward us.

Imagine if, rather than taking to social media, writing sharp blogs about one another, and separating, Christians who disagreed took Communion and worshiped together. What if, rather than defending and sparring, we sidestepped arguments in order to together tell the world of how radically Christ Jesus had changed our lives? This should not just be something we imagine, but something we make a reality.

We do this by following very practical steps like refusing to gossip or slander, being patient and kind to each other, and forgiving one another (Eph. 4:30–32). God wants us to be so committed to Christian unity that we are willing to endure being misunderstood or wronged rather than publicly fighting with each other (see 1 Cor. 6:7–8).

These words bring conviction both to our big picture unity within the Christian community and to our close-knit relationships, including marriage. How easily we divide out of fear and pride instead of enduring with each other.

I can hear your objections even now. "Do we just let people theologically go off the rails? Isn't this how false teachers and bad doctrine infect God's people?"

Jude wrote out of this very concern:

> I felt compelled to write and urge you to contend for the faith that was once for all entrusted to God's holy people. For certain individuals whose condemnation was written about long ago have secretly slipped in among you. They are ungodly people, who pervert the grace of our God into a license for immorality and deny Jesus Christ our only Sovereign and Lord. (Jude 3–4)

Within the family of God, we need to guard our devotion, our core doctrine, and our faith, but even so, do so with a spirit of love.

If the time comes to confront, do so with gentleness with the hope that *God* may lead them to truth and repentance (see 2 Tim. 2:25). Our job is to gently instruct. God's job is to change hearts and minds. Instead of canceling or ignoring a fellow Christian who doesn't change the way you think they should, bear with them, pray for them, and show them unconditional love.

I've noticed that seeking unity within God's family means that I have to surrender my desire to be right. In reality, I have more to learn than I have to teach. Pursuing unity also means that I have to trust that God is big enough to unite and defend His bride without me being the designated "truth monitor."

PRACTICAL WAYS YOU CAN WORK TOWARD UNITY TODAY:

- Initiate a conversation with a Christian with whom you disagree, with the one goal of understanding his or her position. Resist the urge to argue your point.

- Pray regularly for all of the churches and ministries in your town by name.

- When you notice someone criticizing a fellow Christian (in person or online), respond with something positive instead of piling on.

## TRULY SURRENDERED TO LOVE

Throughout this book, we have been on a journey of surrendering the many facets of yourself sexuality represents. Surrendered Identity. Surrendered Thinking. Surrendered Sin. Surrendered Brokenness, Surrendered Idols, and Surrendered Wisdom. But what are you surrendering *to*?

Surrender to love.

In 2008, Francis Chan wrote *Crazy Love*, which became a *New York Times* bestseller.[5] I remember wondering how a book about God's love could be so popular. In my mind, God's love was Christianity 101. Been there, done that. Now let's move on to the meatier and more important parts of the Christian life like theology, sanctification, and ministry.

Just a few years later, the Lord took me through a season in which I began to recognize how little of His love I actually knew. Much of my service and obedience was driven by fear, not by His love. I could accept that Jesus loved me as part of the whole world, but couldn't accept that He loved me, just me. Not because I could offer Him anything, but because He is love. Honestly, this is still a truth I am learning to receive.

God's love was the first thing I learned as a child, but it will also be my very last lesson and greatest measure of maturity. I suspect that when I am one breath away from heaven, ready to let go of this world, my last conscious thought will be of God's love for me. And I believe that when I see Jesus face-to-face, I will be overwhelmed by how little I actually knew of His love here on earth.

We can love only as Jesus pours love through us, overflowing our hearts so that we, like Him, become love. Our love for others is the greatest proof of our own personal relationship with God. A person radically transformed by the love of God will embody that love. We love because He loves us. We forgive because He forgave us. We are patient and gentle only because we are so moved by His great mercy toward us.

Love is the ultimate expression of our surrender. It trusts God to defend, provide, protect, and complete. When I feel like I have to do these things for myself, I cannot love. It is only through a total surrender of the love of God working in me that I can do this.

I can love my neighbor because I'm not worried about fixing the world.

I can love my Christian family because I trust Jesus to guard and refine His bride.

I can love my enemy because I trust Jesus to defend me and protect me.

We love so imperfectly because we have received and surrendered to so little of God's love for us. The only thing that changes us is our surrender to the person of the Lord Jesus Christ.

Paul prayed for fellow believers to know the love of God (Eph. 1:15–23; 3:18–19; 2 Thess. 2:16–17). To seek to personally experience God's love is not a selfish desire, a flighty spiritual experience, or a boring intellectual exercise. It is the very essence of everything it means and is required for Jesus to change everything.

Remember that the enemy's end goal is not to get us to sin, but to keep us from knowing the One whose love sets us free. And so as we end our time together through this book, I ask you, my dear friend, do you know His love? What doubts remain that keep you from trusting Him?

May we strive to know Jesus in such a way that He really does change . . . everything!

## Application Exercise:

---

Love Your Neighbor

Who are the people God has placed in your life who you are to love? How has your agenda gotten in the way of loving your neighbor this week?

Love the Family of God

Share an example of a disagreement you have with a fellow Christian. What does it look like to pursue unity with that person (or group) in spite of this disagreement?

Love Your Enemy

Who is your enemy right now?

How have you been tempted to take revenge or nurture anger towards this person or group?

What does it practically look like to "return a blessing for a curse"?

## Passages to Study:

***Read 1 Peter 3:8–17.***

How does Peter tell us to have an influence in a pagan culture?

How is this advice different from how you have been trying to combat evil in our world?

***Read Ephesians 4:1–6 and 5:1–2.***

List specific ways these verses teach us what it looks like to love other Christians.

How is our love for Christians different than how we are called to love our neighbors?

## Questions for personal reflection and discussion:

1. Do you agree that true godliness will make us people of love? Why or why not?
2. How can our religious agendas get in the way of loving people well? Please share an example of how this has happened in your own life.
3. What does it practically look like for Christians who disagree to return to their common love for Jesus?
4. Why does loving your enemy often look like loving from a distance?
5. How does blessing or praying for your enemy combat evil in the spiritual realm?
6. How does knowing and accepting Jesus's love for you free you to become a loving person?
7. How does your lack of love (for neighbor, friend, or enemy) reveal a deficit in your surrender to God's love for you?

# ACKNOWLEDGMENTS

I am thankful to be part of the Moody Publishers family, many of whom contributed to this book. Special thanks to Judy Dunagan, Erin Davis, Pam Pugh, Connor Sterchi, Kaylee Lockenour Dunn, and Randall Payleitner.

Thank you to many who went through this book, giving me feedback as I was writing, including Troy Loether and Kettlebrook Church, Ian Shire and Providence Church, and Scott Kedersha and Harris Creek Church. Special thanks to the group of ladies who personally journeyed with me, helping me refine as I wrote: Sondra, Laura, Tracy, Allison, Beeaye, Keyla, Elaine, Jaime, Beth, Loe, and Julia. I am also grateful to Zack Verrett and Kate Terry for your ministry with the Brunch group and for helping me refine my writing and teaching. Anna Greer, thank you for helping me get this book to the finish line!

Many from the Authentic Intimacy team and community supported me with prayer and encouragement. None more than my husband and best friend, Mike.

# NOTES

## Chapter 1: What Is Surrendered Sexuality?

1. *Merriam-Webster.com Dictionary*, s.v. "surrender," https://www.merriam-webster.com/dictionary/surrender.

## Chapter 2: Surrendered Identity

1. Abigail Favale, *The Genesis of Gender: A Christian Theory* (Ignatius Press, 2022), 22.
2. Carl R. Trueman, *Strange New World: How Thinkers and Activists Redefined Identity and Sparked the Sexual Revolution* (Crossway, 2022), 71.
3. Casey Shutt, "Pride Month Is a Road to Nowhere," The Gospel Coalition, June 20, 2022, https://www.thegospelcoalition.org/article/pride-month-road-nowhere/.
4. Randy Gilliland and Mikle South, "Shame, Pornography Use, and Relationships: The Impact of Pornography Consumption on Intimacy and Sexual Satisfaction," *Archives of Sexual Behavior* 40, no. 3 (2011): 607–18; and R. C. Reid, J. M. Harper, and E. Anderson, "Shame, Guilt, and Substance Use Among Men with Compulsive Sexual Behavior," *Sexual Addiction & Compulsivity* 21, no. 3 (2014): 255–70.
5. C. S. Lewis, *Mere Christianity* (HarperOne, 2001), 124–25.
6. Tony Reinke, *Newton on the Christian Life: To Live Is Christ* (Crossway, 2015), 49.
7. P. D. Eastman, *Are You My Mother?* (Random House Books for Young Readers, 1960).
8. US Census Bureau, "Children's Living Arrangements" (infographic), November 14, 2023, https://www.census.gov/library/visualizations/interactive/childrens-living-arrangements.html.
9. US Census Bureau, "Calculating Migration Expectancy Using ACS Data," last modified March 28, 2023, accessed October 14, 2024, https://www.census.gov/topics/population/migration/guidance/calculating-migration-expectancy.html.
10. US Department of Health and Human Services, "Our Epidemic of Loneliness and Isolation: The US Surgeon General's Advisory on the Healing Effects of Social Connection and Community," 2023, https://www.hhs.gov/surgeongeneral/priorities/connection/index.html.
11. See, for example, 1 John 3:1; Isaiah 54:5; Psalm 23:1; John 10:11–16; Matthew 10:30; Psalm 139:4; Hebrews 13:5; 1 Corinthians 3:16; John 15:1–17.

12. Jim Wilder and Michael Hendricks, *The Other Half of Church: Christian Community, Brain Science, and Overcoming Spiritual Stagnation* (Moody Publishers, 2020), 28.
13. Pew Research Center, "Religious Landscape Study: Frequency of Prayer," accessed October 6, 2024, https://www.pewresearch.org/religious-landscape-study/database/frequency-of-prayer/. See also Luke 11:1.
14. Rebecca McLaughlin, *No Greater Love: A Biblical Vision for Friendship* (Moody Publishers, 2023), 77.


**Chapter 3: Surrendered Thinking**


1. Brad Wilcox, *Get Married: Why Americans Must Defy the Elites, Forge Strong Families, and Save Civilization* (Broadside Books, 2024), 80.
2. US Department of Health and Human Services, "Our Epidemic of Loneliness and Isolation: The U. S. Surgeon General's Advisory on the Healing Effects of Social Connection and Community," 2023, https://www.hhs.gov/sites/default/files/surgeon-general-social-connection-advisory.pdf. Also see Ernie Mundell, "Rates of Anxiety, Depression Rising Among Americans, Especially the Young," *Health Day,* November 7, 2024, https://www.usnews.com/news/health-news/articles/2024-11-07/rates-of-anxiety-depression-rising-among-americans-especially-the-young.
3. Timothy Keller, *The Meaning of Marriage: Facing the Complexities of Commitment with the Wisdom of God* (Riverhead Books, 2011), 88.
4. Christopher West, *Our Bodies Tell God's Story: Discovering the Divine Plan for Love, Sex, and Gender* (Brazos Press, 2020), 17.
5. See Romans 9:4, Galatians 4:5, and Ephesians 1:5.
6. Sam Allberry, *7 Myths About Singleness* (Crossway, 2019), 120.
7. For further information, see Doug Rosenau, *Single and Sexually Whole: Soulfully Celebrating the Dance of the Sexes* (Sexual Wholeness Resources, 2023), 89–90.
8. Timothy Keller, "Love and Lust," sermon, Redeemer Presbyterian Church, New York City, NY, May 6, 2012, at 9:10–11:31, https://gospelinlife.com/sermon/love-and-lust/.
9. "Moral Issues," Gallup, accessed Sept. 25, 2024, https://news.gallup.com/poll/1681/moral-issues.aspx.
10. Abigail Favale, *The Genesis of Gender: A Christian Theory* (Ignatius Press, 2022), 101.
11. Christopher West, *Theology of the Body for Beginners: A Basic Introduction to Pope John Paul II's Sexual Revolution,* rev. ed. (Ascension Press, 2014), 12.


**Chapter 4: Surrendered Sin**


1. "10 Quotes from Billy Graham about the Cross," The Billy Graham Library, April 3, 2019, https://billygrahamlibrary.org/blog-10-quotes-from-billy-graham-about-the-cross/.
2. Karl Menninger, *Whatever Became of Sin?* (Hawthorn Books, 1973), 24.
3. A. W. Tozer, *The Pursuit of God,* in *The Essential Tozer Collection,* ed. James L. Snyder (Bethany House Publishers, 2017), 87.
4. Blue Letter Bible, "Dictionaries – Repentance," https://www.blueletterbible.org/search/Dictionary/viewTopic.cfm?topic=ET0003105,IT0007368,NT0004116,ST0000166,TT0000475.

5. Dietrich Bonhoeffer, *The Cost of Discipleship* (Touchstone, 1959), 132.
6. Quoted from the ESV® Bible (The Holy Bible, English Standard Version®), © 2001 by Crossway, a publishing ministry of Good News Publishers. Used by permission. All rights reserved.
7. C. S. Lewis, *Mere Christianity* (HarperOne, 2001), 101.

### Chapter 5: Surrendered Brokenness

1. Charlie Health Editorial Team, "How Common Is Sexual Assault? Look at These Statistics," Charlie Health, March 29, 2024, https://www.charliehealth.com/post/sexual-assault-statistics.
2. Tim Hein, *Understanding Sexual Abuse: A Guide for Ministry Leaders and Survivors* (IVP, 2018) 30.
3. Andrea L. Roberts et al., "Does Maltreatment in Childhood Affect Sexual Orientation in Adulthood?" *Archives of Sexual Behavior* 42 (2013): 161–71, https://doi.org/10.1007/s10508-012-0021-9.
4. Justin S. Holcomb and Lindsay A. Holcomb, *Rid of My Disgrace: Hope and Healing for Victims of Sexual Assault* (Crossway, 2011), 106.
5. Dane Ortlund, *Gentle and Lowly: The Heart of Christ for Sinners and Sufferers* (Crossway, 2020), 151–52.
6. Dr. Juli Slattery, *God, Sex, and Your Marriage* (Moody Publishers, 2022).
7. "Trauma," *Psychology Today*, https://www.psychologytoday.com/us/basics/trauma.
8. Dawn McClelland and Chris Gilyard, "Calming Trauma—The Brain and the Limbic System," Phoenix Society for Burn Survivors, August 27, 2019, https://www.phoenix-society.org/resources/calming-trauma.
9. Holcomb and Holcomb, *Rid of My Disgrace*, 74.
10. Curt Thompson, *The Soul of Shame: Retelling the Stories We Believe About Ourselves* (InterVarsity Press, 2015), 30.

### Chapter 6: Surrendered Idols

1. Timothy Keller, *Counterfeit Gods: The Empty Promises of Money, Sex, and Power, and the Only Hope That Matters* (Penguin Books, 2011), xix.
2. Danielle Treweek, *The Meaning of Singleness: Retrieving an Eschatological Vision for the Contemporary Church* (IVP Academic, 2023), 50.
3. Timothy Keller, *Romans 1–7 for You: For Reading, for Feeding, for Leading* (The Good Book Company, 2021), 26.
4. Christopher West, *Theology of the Body for Beginners: Rediscovering the Meaning of Life, Love, Sex, and Gender* (Wellspring, 2018), 30.
5. See Dani Treweek's book *The Meaning of Singleness*, especially pages 43–62 for examples of how this has become the primary narrative in Western church culture. The author shares contempary examples of how single Christians are:
   *Deficient*—"the fundamental determining factor in describing who a single person *is,* is grounded in a description of who they are *not.* The single person is not a husband. They are

not a wife. They are not half of a (married) couple" (43).
*Aberrant* —"Deeply embedded within the evangelical consciousness is a santification narrative which consistenly decipts the married individual as being oriented toward the other-person-centered service while the single person instinctively caters to their egoism and self-centerdness. In this context, any validation of singleness within Christian community is often frowned on as an attempt to justify bad (i.e., sinful) behavior" (47).
*Unfufilled*—"Today's church increasingly regards marriage not as merely a core component of the happy life, but as necessary for anthropological and even spiritual fulfillment. Marriage, we are told, is where a Christian person most closely, intimately and personally encounters God's love for them" (54).

6. Sam Jolman, *The Sex Talk You Never Got: Reclaiming the Heart of Masculine Sexuality* (Thomas Nelson, 2024), 22.
7. C. S. Lewis, *Mere Christianity* (HarperOne, 2001), 100.
8. Some of these ministries are:
   Pure Desire Ministries: https://puredesire.org
   Be Broken Ministries: https://bebroken.org
   The Samson Society (for Christian men "who are serious about authenticity, community, humility, and Recovery"): https://samsonsociety.com
   Celebrate Recovery ("a safe place to find freedom from your hurts, hangups, and habits"): https://celebraterecovery.com
9. Rebecca McLaughlin, *No Greater Love: A Biblical Vision for Friendship* (Moody Publishers, 2023), 32.
10. For example, Sam Allberry, Rebecca McLaughlin, Dani Treweek, Christopher Yuan, Brownlyn Lee, Rachel Gilson, Kutter Calloway.
11. Joshua Brown and Joel Wong, "How Gratitude Changes You and Your Brain," *Greater Good Magazine*, June 6, 2017, https://greatergood.berkeley.edu/article/item/how_gratitude_changes_you_and_your_brain.
12. Linda Dillow, *Satisfy My Thirsty Soul: A Woman's Guide to Deeper Intimacy with God* (NavPress, 2021), 201–202.
13. Matt Maher, "Lord, I Need You," *All the People Said Amen* (Essential Records, 2013), https://genius.com/Matt-maher-lord-i-need-you-lyrics.

### Chapter 7: Surrendered Wisdom

1. Debra Fileta (@debrafileta), "When we make dating about intimacy, we get confused really fast," Instagram, June 29, 2022, https://www.instagram.com/debrafileta/p/CfZTa-oL-ON/.
2. The Message, copyright © 1993, 2002, 2018 by Eugene H. Peterson. Used by permission of NavPress. All rights reserved. Represented by Tyndale House Publishers, a Division of Tyndale House Ministries.
3. Repurposed from Juli Slattery, "Is It OK to Masturbate?," Boundless.org, April 22, 2024, https://www.boundless.org/adulthood/is-it-ok-to-masturbate/.
4. Neil A. Bradbury, "All Cells Have a Sex: Sex Chromosome Function at the Cellular Level," in *Principles of Gender-Specific Medicine*, 4th ed., ed. Marianne J. Legato (Academic Press,

2023), 213–64.

5. Juli Slattery, "Juli & Jackie on How to Pursue Unity While Standing on Truth," episode 375, *Java with Juli* (podcast), August 23, 2001, 39 min., 2 sec., https://www.authenticintimacy.com/375-juli-jackie-on-how-to-pursue-unity-while-standing-on-truth/.
6. Juli Slattery, *Finding the Hero in Your Husband, Revisited: Embracing Your Power in Marriage* (Health Communications Inc., 2021).
7. I have read a number of books over the years that have helped me understand a more thorough and biblical understanding of gender. Here are a few I would recommend if you want to read more:
   *Love Thy Body: Answering Hard Questions About Life and Sexuality* by Nancy Pearcey;
   *The Genesis of Gender: A Christian Theory* by Abigail Favale;
   *Fully Alive: A Biblical Vision of Gender That Frees Men and Women to Live Beyond Stereotypes* by Larry Crabb;
   *Neither Complementarian nor Egalitarian: A Kingdom Corrective to the Evangelical Gender Debate* by Michelle Lee-Barnewall.
8. You will find resources you can trust at authenticintimacy.com, including videos, online book studies, podcasts, books, and more.

**Chapter 8: Surrendered to Love**

1. Linda Kay Klein, *Pure: Inside the Evangelical Movement that Shamed a Generation of Young Women and How I Broke Free* (Atria Books, 2018), 201.
2. The transcript of Rachael Denhollander's statement can be found here (CNN, updated January 30, 2018): https://www.cnn.com/2018/01/24/us/rachael-denhollander-full-statement/index.html.
3. *Merriam-Webster.com Dictionary*, s.v. "unity," https://www.merriam-webster.com/dictionary/unity.
4. Francis Chan, *Until Unity* (David C Cook, 2021), 55.
5. Francis Chan, *Crazy Love: Overwhelmed by a Relentless God* (David C Cook, 2008).

Java
with Juli
WITH DR. JULI SLATTERY

More books from Dr. Juli Slattery to help you make sense of God and sex.